As Tough as Necessary

Countering Violence, Aggression, and Hostility in Our Schools

Richard L. Curwin
Allen N. Mendler

Association for Supervision and Curriculum Development
Alexandria, Virginia

Association for Supervision and Curriculum Development
1250 N. Pitt Street   Alexandria, Virginia 22314-1453
Telephone: 1-800-933-2723 or 703-549-9110 Fax: 703-299-8631

Gene R. Carter, *Executive Director*
Michelle Terry, *Assistant Executive Director, Program Development*
Ronald S. Brandt, *Assistant Executive Director*
Nancy Modrak, *Director, Publishing*
John O'Neil, *Acquisitions Editor*
Julie Houtz, *Managing Editor of Books*
René Bahrenfuss, *Associate Editor*
Kathie Felix, *Associate Editor*
Gary Bloom, *Director, Design, Editorial, and Production Services*
Karen Monaco, *Senior Designer*
Tracey A. Smith, *Production Coordinator*
Dina Murray, *Production Assistant*
Valerie Sprague, *Desktop Publisher*

Printed in the United States of America.

s6/97
ASCD Stock No.: 197017
ASCD member price: $12.95   nonmember price: $15.95

Library of Congress Cataloging-in-Publication Data
Curwin, Richard L., 1944-
    As tough as necessary : countering violence, aggression, and
    hostility in our schools / Richard L. Curwin, Allen N. Mendler.
        p. cm.
    Includes bibliographical references (p.).
    ISBN 0-87120-280-8 (pbk.)
        1. School violence—United States. 2. School violence—United
    States—Prevention. 3. Schools—United States—Safety measures.
    4. Classroom management—United States. 5. School management and
    organization—United States. I. Mendler, Allen N. II. Title.
    LB3013.3.C89 1997
       371.7'82—dc21   97-18652
                                                              CIP

01 00 99 98 97   5 4 3 2 1

To Elliot and Joyce Curwin, my brother and sister, who with me shared sorrow, joy, the fulfillment of dreams, and through it all, hope. Each found success in a unique way, without compromise, and taught me to never give up.

—*Richard L. Curwin*

To my main sources of support, encouragement, enrichment, and love: my wife Barbara, for 25 wonderful years, and our children Jason, Brian, and Lisa. I can only hope that this book contributes to making the world a little safer for you and those you love.

—*Allen N. Mendler*

Acknowledgments

We would like to thank everyone below for their contributions:

David Curwin for his helpful and timely research.

Mark Goldberg for his painstaking editorial work and his encouragement, support, and sharing of himself.

Ron Brandt and the staff at ASCD for their continued support of our work, especially to Kathie Felix and Julie Houtz for their meticulous editing of our manuscript and to Karen Monaco for designing the powerful emotion-evoking cover for this book.

Gil Scott-Heron, for his inspiration in overcoming his personal demons. With the recording *Spirits*, his music opened the door for us to understand "the spirits calling" that all children need to hear to find life-fulfilling alternatives to destruction.

Elizabeth Osta with the Rochester City School District for her committed support of *Discipline with Dignity* and, most importantly, her selfless devotion to antiviolence efforts in her community.

Frank Koontz at the Bureau of Education and Research for his insights and patience in helping us communicate our message more effectively to fellow educators.

Tammy Rowland, our able program manager, for her research and her highly competent handling of nuts-and-bolts issues, which gave us the time we needed to concentrate on writing.

Teri Segal and Samantha Noonan for their research and information control.

Alan Blankstein and staff at the National Educational Service for their long-term commitment, creativity, and devotion to programs for at-risk kids, including the publication of two of our books and two video programs.

Phil Harris at Phi Delta Kappa for his friendship and treasured advice.

Otis for his unconditional love and patience while I was writing.

Our magnificent team of associates including Susan Strauss, Dave and Colleen Zawadzki, Willeta Corbett, Ivy Lovelady, Mary Ann Evans-Patrick, Esther Wright, and Beverly White.

All the students, teachers, administrators, and counselors who contributed letters, insights, and suggestions to this work.

All the schools, administrators, teachers, and parents who have allowed us to work with them, meet their children, learn their problems, seek solutions, and gather advice.

As Tough as Necessary

*Countering Violence, Aggression, and
Hostility in Our Schools*

A Letter from the Authors

Naming books often requires as much skill as writing them. The title of our last ASCD publication, *Discipline With Dignity*, accurately captured the core of our message: a discipline process that maintains dignity for students and educators alike while also teaching students how to behave responsibly. This concept reflected our belief that the most important "R" of school always has been and always will be responsibility. The book (and the title) struck a chord with readers and became one of the most successful discipline programs in the United States, as well as one of ASCD's best-selling books.

The title of this book, *As Tough as Necessary*, does not reflect a hardening against our position on the way difficult children should be treated. We do not mean to say, "Get tough with the little brats, as tough as necessary to get them to behave." Instead, we hope that the title reflects the firmness of our belief in finding a variety of ways to help aggressive, hostile, and violent children learn alternatives to hurting others.

In this title, we promote three precise notions that form the heart and soul of the book:

1. Change is tough. Changing behavior is the single most difficult task humans face within their lifetime: changing the nature of a violent society full of negative images, a dehumanized world struggling to recapture the power of altruism, media excited and fueled by hostility, and a politicized world where killing and hurting are just as often cheered and praised as rejected.

We need to develop a toughness, a resilience, if we are to accomplish the hard work of reducing the influence of violence on children. We need to get tough with ourselves—as tough as necessary—even if that means abandoning teaching methods that once worked but now compound our problems. We must resolve to use more appropriate methods of dealing with feelings of aggression and hostility.

2. "As tough as necessary" is not the same as "zero tolerance."
Policies of zero tolerance for misbehavior were created with noble
intentions to prevent athletes, children of influence, and others who
manipulated the system to get away with rule breaking. We whole-
heartedly support the goal of the policy. Unfortunately, zero tolerance
has been reframed as a simplistic justification for treating every problem with one solution. Schools once claimed to use zero tolerance as a
statement of their commitment to respond aggressively to the intolera-
ble. Now the words too often are an excuse to punish without
thought, to remove the troublemakers without guilt or responsibility,
or to sound tough without doing the tough work of finding real solutions.

"As tough as necessary" is the conceptual opposite of zero tolerance. It means "do what works." Getting tough is okay as long as it is
necessary. Our extensive work in school discipline over 15 years has
proven to us that behavior and problems worsen when the solutions
or consequences are based on formulas rather than circumstances,
motivations, and needs. The motivation for behavior and the way students make choices are the central factors that should determine the
selection of consequences to teach responsibility. We must be as tough
as necessary to dismiss once and for all the simplistic and erroneous
belief that all children can be treated the same when they behave the
same. Children's education and their process of socialization is too
important to trivialize in that way.

**3. Violence prevention and intervention require thoughtful
educators who are willing to make tough choices.** Policies like zero
tolerance trivialize educators by making the system foolproof, implying
that even a fool can do it. We believe that education is the most
important profession in our culture, and that most teachers make
good decisions with experience, time to think, support from the community, and freedom to make an occasional mistake without fear of
unreasonable consequences.

As professional educators, we must act in ways that strengthen the
profession. We must be as tough as necessary to counter politicians,
community groups, radical fanatics, and others who wish to remove
our ability and responsibility to do what is best for children and society. We must also be as tough as necessary with ourselves by removing
inadequate teachers, by providing the best training possible for every-

one involved with children, and by working with all groups to find common solutions to the problems of violence that threaten us.

Those who have attended our training sessions and seminars, as well as those who have read our previous books, know our style of sharing experiences through personal stories and real-life anecdotes. Although this book was written by two authors, many of the anecdotes in the book are related by a single narrator. We hope you'll appreciate the potency and immediacy of hearing stories told from this point of view.

RICK CURWIN
San Francisco, California

ALLEN MENDLER
Rochester, New York

Introduction

At different times, each of the authors of this book has visited Jerusalem and the Holocaust Museum called Yad Vashem. Our discussion of our experiences there turned solemn when we relived the horror of visiting the Children's Memorial, which honors the two million children murdered in the Holocaust. Our sadness and compassion stretched all the way from Nazi Germany (and in reality, several centuries before that) into the future. We mourned for all the children who are and will be victims of violence, and we raged against the forces that hurt them.

Our thoughts inevitably focused on what might be called a wholesale destruction of U.S. children, a destruction whose scope is great enough to evoke a despair similar to what we felt at the steps of the Children's Memorial. Unlike the Holocaust, no single group in the United States is singling out others and committing genocide. But the randomness of violence and the permeating fear are tragic not only for their numbing impact on children today but also for the way they damage our hope for the future.

Consider the fact that in 1993, gunfire was the fourth leading cause of death for children between the ages of 5 and 9, right after accidents, cancer, and birth defects. For 10- to 14-year-olds, gunfire was the second leading cause of death. Among 15- to 19-year-olds, black males were shot at the rate of 153.1 per 1,000; the rate was 28.8 for white males. In general, gunfire deaths have increased for youth over the last 10 years. Between 1992 and 1993 alone, the rate of increase was 7 percent.[1] This is to say nothing about the increase in nonhomicidal violence and the growth in the numbers of gangs, gang members, and the havoc they cause.

In 1996, a group of three youngsters aged 6, 5, and 5 inexplicably beat a month-old baby to near death. While this aberration does not

---

[1]Statistics from the Children's Defense Fund, 1996.

reflect an increase in "pediatric gangs," it does demonstrate a radical lowering of age for violent offenders. Only a year earlier, a group of 10-year-olds beat a 6-year-old to death, and in Chicago a youngster was thrown off a building by youths not even 12 years old. On a daily basis, schools face other less spectacular, but still unacceptable, increases in fights, threats, and vandalism.

This book is our prayer and our response to the increase in violence. We hope to alter the path by slowing down, if not ending, the tragedy of violence in our own time, in our own country, in our own world, and for all our own children.

Many children in the United States have short attention spans. Most of the blame is attributed to the media, especially fast-paced television and other entertainment. Little recognition is given to the influence of adults and their short attention spans when they interact with children. Especially disturbing is the juxtaposition of our deep grief when children suffer against the short time we pay attention to the tragedy. Our lives are filled with the horror du jour; each day we forget yesterday's headline.

Equally disturbing is the profile of the children for whom we choose to grieve. Most are white, middle class, and cute. Consider Polly Klaas, abducted from her own bedroom and killed. Or remember Alex and Michael Smith, drowned by their mother. There are the children in Oklahoma City, represented by Christian Bramble, whose moving poem, "I Am the Voice of the Children," touched the entire nation.

All of these children certainly deserve our grief. Their situations demand our anger, and we need to be inspired by them to find solutions to the monstrous consequences of violence. Yet have you heard of Kierra and Cierra Kidd of Monroeville, Alabama? They were killed by their father for insurance money in November of 1993. One wonders if the fact that they are African American children has anything to do with why their story never made national news or captured the public heart.

Now it is time for us to grieve for all our children. They are dying in too many ways: spiritually, intellectually, psychologically, culturally, and physically. They are children of every color and class, the ones who never make the news. They fill our streets, malls, and schools. And our inspiration to take action on their behalf must last longer than a day. It requires a commitment over time, a commitment to the belief that all children have value and every act of violence against them is a crime against our way of life, our most important values, and our belief in our future.

This book was written with the lofty goal and fervent hope that our children can be saved from the enemy within. Violence bred on aggression and hostility is eating away at the core of our country as well as so many others, transforming it into a land that is unrecognizable as what most postwar children dreamed about for their children. What can and should schools do about this problem?

Our answer is that we should do as much as humanly possible. The curriculum of the 21st century must include skills in how to get along with each other, which is as close to the basics as a society can ever hope to get. Without these skills and knowledge, no other learning will matter much. The enemy within will overtake and overpower us. We are already losing ground, but this book offers hope and encouragement. We have seen how effective programs can change the way children think and behave. Schools can and should lead the way to a safer and saner future.

The Structure of This Book

Chapter 1 discusses the problem we face. It considers how violence, aggression, and hostility have affected our society and our schools—and our educational imperative to confront them. The chapter offers perspective on school violence and discusses attitudes toward possible remedies.

Chapter 2 considers changing schools so they promote, model, value, and teach according to principles and values. It recommends removing violent interventions that promote aggression and hostility. It also recommends making nonviolent values the center of the entire school operating system. The chapter offers a perspective on how a lack of values rather than a lack of punishments has contributed to the problem of violence.

Chapter 3 outlines strategies for teachers to use to help students change their choices about aggressive feelings. These strategies address ways to perceive, treat, and teach students. The chapter focuses on school and classroom procedures for controlling violent student behavior, diffusing potentially violent situations, and teaching alternatives to violence.

Chapter 4 describes specific ways for students to control aggression and nonviolent choices for resolving problems. These include strategies for controlling aggression and hostility, meeting basic needs in nonviolent ways, and getting along with each other. This chapter offers a curriculum for students as well as strategies for teachers.

Chapter 5 offers specific short- and long-term steps to make schools safer from violence. It examines immediate safety issues facing schools and 25 ways to approach them.

We sincerely hope and believe that schools can and will take a stand against the violence that rages against our children and dims the light that should illuminate their future. Schools worldwide as well as in the United States can have no more significant mission than to identify, define, and act in every possible way to end the wholesale destruction threatening not only the democratic way of life, but all life.

The Problem of Violence

We all have seen an increase in aggression and hostility in the United States as well as worldwide, and the rate of that increase is itself growing. The causes for such violence are many: economic malaise; cynicism about the political process; drugs; gangs; the entertainment media; and the breakdown of the family. Too many children have been overly rewarded and punished and, most important, not taught values.

Schools have an imperative to face these problems directly and squarely for two reasons. The first is that schools themselves are threatened by increased violence. Students cannot learn and teachers cannot teach when fear for one's person, possessions, and self-concept runs rampant. Second, schools are responsible for teaching students the skills needed to maintain and advance our culture. Learning to deal with aggression and hostility in nonviolent ways is as important, if not more so, than anything else in the curriculum.

Violence, Aggression, And Hostility

Since the 1988 publication of our book *Discipline with Dignity*, we have conducted thousands of workshops and seminars, trained staff members in several schools, and visited many others to offer consultation. In the last five years, especially, we have observed several trends.

- There are more behaviorally disruptive students than ever
  before, and the rate is increasing.
- Children are becoming more disruptive at younger ages. What
  were once exclusively high school misbehaviors have reached
  the primary grades.
- Children are more violent, and teens are especially prone to
  violence. They are 2.5 times as likely to suffer an incident of
  violence than those over age 20 (Licitra 1993).
- Many children lack any sense of caring or remorse.
- Students are increasingly described by those who educate them
  as aggressive and hostile.

When the movie *The Breakfast Club* came out in 1985, most teachers dreaded students like the tough character named Bender, whose short fuse combined with a simmering anger to make him confrontational and oppositional. Within five years, however, many teachers viewed the Benders of the world as more "troubled" than dangerous. Given the behavior of truly hostile students, Bender was more or less acceptable. Today, nearly all teachers have students far more dangerous than Bender.

In less than a decade, the fear of a switchblade has been replaced with the fear of a semiautomatic machine gun with laser sights. Nothing better illustrates the increase in violence, aggression, and hostility than our gradual acceptance of what was once unacceptable misbehavior. In fact, the limits of what is acceptable are being stretched beyond reason. Whereas talking back to the teacher and using foul language used to be acts that sent a student to the principal's office or even detention, such behaviors are now expected. Moreover, they are accompanied by students' increasing unwillingness to work on school projects and, perhaps most disheartening, an erosion of remorse for disruptive behavior.

The strain, fear, and bewilderment these conditions generate in educators and students significantly interferes with teaching and learning. Violence has reduced our world so that we are afraid to allow our children to walk outside at night, we are afraid to let them play on their own without supervision, and we invest more and more financial resources to protect ourselves and our possessions.

Liberty and freedom cannot exist in a society permeated by fear. We are our own greatest enemy—and we are armed and dangerous.

The Challenges We Face

Most of the disruptive children described above come from troubled homes. Some studies indicate that as many as 80 percent of disruptive children come from dysfunctional homes (Herbert 1994). We can do little to improve these families, but we must remember that our students of today are the parents of tomorrow. If we don't take strong, positive, meaningful measures to change how these students function as parents, what will their children be like? Schools have both the opportunity and the responsibility to respond.

Politicians from both the right and left continually use phrases like "traditional" or "family" values, meaning a return to the beliefs of simpler, "more moral" times. Whether or not the past was as ideal as its mythology suggests, we need a vision for tomorrow, not yesterday. As family structures change, so must the way values are taught and demonstrated. Right and wrong are timeless concepts, and hurting others never has been and never will be acceptable. How do we teach children that hurting others is wrong? What does hurting others mean? How does defending our possessions, bodies, and dignity differ from committing an unacceptable aggressive act?

We believe schools must accept this mandate and make it a major part of their mission: to help students become less violent by learning how to control their aggression. What follows in this book are structures and techniques designed to help prevent violent attitudes and behaviors along with ways to respond when they do occur.

As we encountered more questions and problems related to violence and its effect on learning, *Discipline with Dignity* evolved to address those concerns. It became our professional challenge to comprehend the true nature of violence without labeling or blaming, to discover what can be done about violence, and to determine what schools can and should realistically do given all their other responsibilities. We feel excitement in discovering how naturally *Discipline with Dignity* provides a genuine, comprehensive, and practical framework without resorting to simplistic solutions or formulas.[1] Before we look at that framework, let's first examine in detail the problems that challenge the prevention of violence.

---

[1]This book is based on the principles and applications of *Discipline With Dignity*. It is not a revision of that book but an application of its principles. Reading *Discipline With Dignity* will enhance your understanding of this book; not reading it, however, will not hamper you in applying what you learn through reading this book.

Humans Are Violent

Aggression is part of human nature. Some researchers believe it is chemically built into our genes. History proves that human violence against humans is not a postmodern, 20th century invention. Genocides, serial killings, thefts, and gang (turf) wars terrified—and attracted—our ancestors. Our modern entertainment media are no more violent than pretechnology art and literature. The Grimm brothers' fairy tales are explicitly violent, and Edgar Allan Poe's tales of terror frightened readers without any mention of assault weapons.

So violence isn't new, and some data indicate a decrease over the last 10 years in both the number and percentage of murders, muggings, robberies, and rapes (Herbert 1994). Why, then, is there a sudden emergency, a seemingly national obsession to end violence? And why are we more terrified by aggression than ever before?

Violence today feels different—more heartless, more senseless, and more random. We are confronted by aggression and hostility without remorse or even reason. The phenomenon of, "It won't happen to me!" has been replaced with, "They're after me!" At one time a person might have been murdered for money; now it might be for wearing the wrong hat. It seems as if we are all wearing targets on our backs, even inside the "safety" of our homes. Headlines about drive-by shootings and kidnappings of children have not only sparked calls for tougher laws but have increased our perceived need to safeguard ourselves from the "bad guys." Even worse, the bad guys don't need to infiltrate our neighborhoods. They now live next door to us, or in the same home.

How pervasive is violence? Statistics paint a confusing picture. If the general numbers do not reveal an overall increase in violent incidents, they do tell us that violence against children is rapidly increasing and that youngsters are in serious peril. Can it really be true that 14 U.S. children and teenagers are killed by a gunshot wound every day (Herbert 1994). Can there really be somewhere between 100,000 and 200,000 guns brought to school each day (Licitra 1993)? Is it true that juvenile arrests for violent crime increased 11.8 percent in suburban areas—and 17.7 percent in rural communities from 1990 to 1991 (Licitra 1993)? Is it possible that thousands of kids from all socioeconomic groups in urban, suburban, and rural areas from coast to coast belong to gangs?

Sadly, violence is as much a reality in schools as it is in society. And yet the school remains the safest sanctuary for many children confronted with daily assaults to their physical and psychological well-being. Still, the last few years have seen an explosion in books, articles, programs, community and school initiatives, and laws designed to curb the problem of school violence and the social aggression that leads to it. From metal detectors to conflict resolution programs, permanent police officers on campus to zero tolerance, alternative schools to expulsion, educators are struggling to come to grips with a problem that threatens to undermine the instructional initiatives needed to transform schools into the technologically sophisticated institutions demanded by today's workplace.

What Is Violence?

We define violence as an assault to one's person that can take three forms: body (physical injury), esteem (verbal harassment such as name calling), or property (damage to things one owns). Violence is bred in an atmosphere of hostility and aggression where it feels and looks better to hurt than to resolve and tolerate. The image of a hero as one who escalates aggression and conquers is pervasive, while the image of the hero as one who stays calm and finds real solutions is nearly nonexistent. All educators realize that learning is seriously affected when children and teachers feel unsafe. Learning cannot flourish when students are worried about being hurt, being put-down, or having things they value defaced or destroyed.

The causes of violence are complex and often interwoven. Abused children grow up to be abusive adults who perpetuate a cycle of violence directed towards those they can victimize—and two to three million children are reportedly abused in this country each year. Other causes include the continuing erosion of the nurturing family structure, the absence of fathers, increasing depersonalization within communities, and a diminishing impact of community values.

For those who do not feel the nurturing influence of a healthy family life, gangs become a substitute family. Others join gangs out of fear or for the excitement they envision. Gang members used to "rumble" with switchblades. Now, with incredibly easy access to handguns and combat weapons, shootings are common. The leading cause of death for black and white boys of all ages is gunshot wounds; in fact, firearms kill more youth between the ages of 15 and 24 than all other natural causes combined (Herbert 1994).

The media present a picture of shooting as a natural way of living, barraging impressionable youth with images of death and violence. The typical U.S. household has its television set on for 7 hours a day, and children aged 2 to 11 spend an average of 28 hours a week watching; by age 18, the average child will have viewed 200,000 acts of violence on television (Murray n.d.).

In addition, commercials promote the acquisition of quick and easy goods and status, as do high profile sports stars and team owners who demand—and receive—staggering amounts of money. The actions of these highly visible personalities do not teach loyalty and stability. Drugs are viewed as a viable or even preferable economic and lifestyle option to many who are financially and emotionally impoverished. For those who see others with money and have little or no prospect of "getting theirs," drugs offer fast cash. Dealers flash money as part of their advertising pitch. The short life associated with drug-related activity is irrelevant to those who don't care, and if some can't make money at it, they try to reassure themselves with the thought that using drugs makes poverty and hopelessness bearable—or at least temporarily forgettable.

Technology generates as many problems as it solves by creating an impersonal set of obstacles to human contact. Many people now prefer to reach an answering machine than to talk to another person over the phone because they find it is easier to leave a message than to converse. Dating on the Internet allows us to be anything we want: clear-skinned, thin, funny, safe. Sending an e-mail message is quick and easy, but it subtly affects our ability to communicate directly with other human beings and to better understand and accept ourselves. An e-mail message lacks the nonverbal cues that are part of face-to-face communication—tone of voice, eye contact, the tilt of the head, gestures. Without those nonverbal cues, we may very often misconstrue what's being said in the message that pops up on our computer screens. Many people do just that, and the result is electronic violence—"flaming."

Many of us are sick and tired of "understanding" all of these causes of violence. We find ourselves longing for a return to a simpler and saner time when authority figures were the good guys to be respected.

We are outraged when school boards have to debate whether to buy metal detectors or textbooks. Disrespectful graffiti slogans that lead to budget allocations for new paint and belt sanders offend our sense of right and wrong and make us want to fight back. These feelings of frustration can lead to simplistic solutions that make us feel momentarily empowered—but no safer. All of us must push beyond our anger if we are to really make a difference.

There aren't enough in-school suspension, time-out, or planning rooms to accommodate these numbers. If we expel a student from school who then creates havoc at the shopping mall, who then influences them? Have we done anything more than displace a danger from one location to the next? It is not enough to fortify the gates of the school. We can be far more successful by transforming schools into places that teach children to control their violent nature, to reduce aggressive and hostile attitudes and behaviors that lead to violence, and to change a self-destructive path.

What Can Schools Do?

When social problems reach Main Street, schools are asked to fix them. Why should educators add violence to the myriad other social ills they are asked to cure? Even if most students are not chronically hostile, those who are cause fear and disruption for everyone else. What can we do about the problem when our society itself seems powerless? We cannot do everything, but we'd better do something. For too many children, school is their only chance. And so we must deal not only with the impact of angry, frustrated children, but we must address the causes of violence in working towards its prevention.

In *Discipline with Dignity*, we proposed a model of discipline that teaches students how to behave responsibly while emphasizing the enhancement of self-esteem and the requisite skills of social problem solving and self-regulation as serious components of curriculum and instruction. We advocate the idea that behavior and the ability to choose how to behave must be taught like all other aspects of the curriculum and that every educator has a responsibility to be actively involved.

In this book we apply the principles of *Discipline with Dignity* to the problems of violence, aggression, and hostility. It has been designed to provide insights and practical methodologies for educators to offer students caring, concern, dignity, respect, and tolerance. This book describes practical methods of **prevention**: things educators can do to minimize the likelihood that students will act in aggressive ways at school. We provide many methods of **action**: ways of behaving and communicating with students when they are engaging in challenging, potentially explosive behaviors. We also describe skills that students can learn to make them better at identifying "anger triggers" so they can choose alternatives to violent responses. Finally, we offer ideas of **resolution**: ways to deal with particularly difficult youth who provoke crises on a regular basis. This three-dimensional approach has been very effective in helping thousands of educators establish effective discipline practices in their classrooms.

Essential Beliefs for Effective Prevention

The following beliefs underlie effective violence prevention, and programs cannot sustain long-term progress without them.

Strategies must be practical. We define practical by how effective they are, not by how easy or fast they may be. Fast, easy solutions are never practical if they are not effective. If they do not decrease hostile or aggressive behavior, do not use them.

Not all confrontations are violent or unhealthy. Students learn how to handle confrontations only by experiencing them and learning from that experience. In that sense, certain types of confrontations should be encouraged rather than outlawed. We often hear from middle school teachers they dread fights involving girls more than they do fights involving boys because the girls' fights are a relatively new phenomenon and take unpredictable forms, whereas boys' fights have been happening for years and teachers usually understand how the fight is going to play out. That's a problem because 45 percent of 8- to 12-year-old girls were involved in an incident of violent behavior in the last year (Stepp 1992). Perhaps girls lack the benefits of learning how to be confrontational in their early years because of sex stereotyping: "Nice girls don't fight." All children can learn that there are legitimate things to be angry about and that there are nonaggressive ways to handle anger.

The core strategies and interventions are based primarily on values, rather than rewards or punishments. Violence prevention programs are only effective when students choose to be nonviolent in the absence of authority. Rewards and punishment teach the opposite. The salient value is that hurting others is wrong, as opposed to, "I'll get in trouble if I hurt another," or, just as harmful, "I'll get a reward if I stop." We may choose to use rewards for short-term benefit, but long-term change is fueled by methods that teach and reinforce proper values like safety, altruism, caring, respect, and—most important, remorse.

All behaviors that we want students to choose must be modeled, taught, and retaught by everyone in the school. In his book *Emotional Intelligence*, Goleman (1995) notes that the ability to recognize a feeling is the key to emotional intelligence. We are important adults in the lives of challenging students, and we must become vigilant in recognizing our own feelings of frustration. These feelings must be processed in a way that keeps us in our "adult" state. Most importantly, when we express frustration, it must model respect, dignity, and nonviolence. We must repeatedly show how to use the tools that we want students to develop.

Each and every student is welcomed by the school, even when he or she misbehaves. There can be no students or groups who are marginalized or considered less valued than others. We need to teach and demonstrate the principle that no life can be wasted or devalued. Misbehavior requires consequences, and they may occasionally feel miserable as long as they are offered as a caring parent would correct, not like the criminal justice system.

Everyone in the school is involved with both the creation and implementation of the violence prevention program. This includes students, teachers, administrators, aides, the bus driver, and lunchroom supervisors. Without a schoolwide commitment, no change will last.

Effective violence prevention requires transcending the political arena, including political correctness and especially "political incorrectness." Words like liberal, conservative, permissive, and religious right are inapplicable and destructive. Politics that polarize create blame, offer simplistic understandings, and a need to win. These

breed hostility that causes more violence. Values that are necessary to
the fulfillment of educational goals should be taught in school. Vocal
minorities that object to the teaching of values should be heard and
respected but neither feared nor revered. No matter how intimidating
the messenger may be, we cannot back down from what is right for
our culture and for our children.

A Schoolwide Approach

We advocate a comprehensive schoolwide approach to violence prevention that includes three basic components and provides specific,
practical strategies. These are:

**1. Teach students skills to be less violent, aggressive, and hos-
tile.** Students behave violently as a way of satisfying one or more of
their basic needs. They may be expressing anger or frustration, showing off, seeking a sense of control, or protecting themselves.
Throughout their lives, children have learned how to express their
feelings by observing their parents and teachers, as well as the Power
Rangers, Roseanne, Bart Simpson, and Beavis and Butt-Head. The
more tools students have to choose from to meet their needs and to
express their feelings, the greater the likelihood they will use them.

Many of the methods of *Discipline with Dignity* teach alternatives
to violence. Conflict resolution, peer mediation, and anger control are
examples of existing programs that teach students nonviolent ways to
settle disputes and meet their needs. We can teach students positive
skills both for preventing disruptive events and for dealing with the
consequences of violent encounters.

2. Teach students how to make more effective choices. Once
students have additional skills, they need to know when to use them
and how to choose among them. Every time a student breaks a rule or
behaves disruptively, he or she needs both firm limits and significant
choices. Firm limits show that we mean business about what we will
and will not accept. Significant choices help students realize that they
are capable of selecting nonviolent alternatives. For example, "You
have chosen to give yourself a time out (limit). Come back when you
are ready to learn (choice)."

3. Model for students alternative expressions of anger, frustration, and impatience. School personnel—including teachers, administrators, counselors, lunchroom monitors, and school bus drivers— need to model the same choices and behaviors that they want their students to use. No student can ever do what he or she has never seen. By using the same skills and making positive choices, we show students that real people use nonviolent strategies and that they work, even when people feel hostile.

For example, fighting students' disrespect with sarcasm and removing them from the classroom validates the very same student behavior we seek to change. It is best to respond in the same manner expected of the student when he or she is angry: "I don't like it when you make fun of me, but I can understand that you might be angry or embarrassed. Let's talk later and see if we can work it out."

Keys to Dealing with School and Classroom Violence

The following principles provide the structure for the *Discipline with Dignity* approach to school and classroom aggression, hostility, and violence.

Teaching Student Behavior Is Part of the Job

Many teachers are frustrated with the growing demands placed upon them to be all things to all students. So it is understandable that demands for teaching social skills, peacemaking, and conflict mediation are met with skepticism and diffidence. Many educators prefer quick formulas that specify what to do when students engage in behavior that is harmful or inappropriate to the learning process. And yet, the complexity of human behavior defies simplistic solutions. That is why every program that lists a sequential format of how to teach or discipline all students is doomed to failure.

Let's learn from the past and recognize that it has taken most students a long time to develop anger, hostility, and aggression. Turning things around is no easy quest and requires the commitment of all responsible adults. Preventing violence takes time and a serious commitment.

We Must Create and Nurture Community Networks

It is no longer possible for teachers to meet the learning needs of all students in a typical classroom. And with the growth of inclusion, the diversity of learning needs is greater than ever. No matter how talented, a single teacher cannot simultaneously teach five reading groups, manage four students with Attention Deficit Hyperactive Disorder (ADHD), facilitate a conflict mediation between two upset children, and take an autistic child for a walk. In recognition of this diversity, educators, particularly classroom teachers, must create a network of resources to meet students' needs. Parents, senior citizens, and volunteers can be called on to help make a difference in students' lives. Individual volunteers, as well as civic-minded community and business organizations, need to be recruited.

After turning his own life around, ex-convict and youth service worker Kenneth Barksdale has committed himself to sparing young people the harsher lessons of life that he learned the hard way. In his talks to young people in trouble, he describes hearing his own mother tell him, "You're just like your %$#&^* father." Barksdale hated everyone, "cops, my father, my mother. All of my life I was told I wouldn't live to see my 14th birthday. . . . But deep down inside, I wanted someone to hold me, tell me I was special. I wanted the attention I never got when I was home." After powerfully connecting with the kids, Barksdale asks for and gives individual hugs to his listeners.

The Rochester Rotary Club provides an example of how a school's affiliation with one civic-minded community organization can make a difference. This organization "adopted" an inner-city school. They donated coats and sweaters for students and children's books for the library. Also, they have taken the children on a variety of trips into the community. Barry Culhane, cochair of the Rotary Club's Community Service Committee, says, "The idea was to concentrate our support in one school and to make a difference. We went through a process of looking for a particular school to help. We needed to get our arms around a school and really hug the children tightly and make sure they knew us."

A Rochester, New York, based company, Frontier Corp., has adopted an "at-risk" 3rd grade class and donated $120,000, which has paid for a wide range of services such as before- and after-school programs, field trips, and a four-week summer camp. Some money was used to hire two social workers to help the families of the 29 pupils. After one year, attendance, behavior, and performance of these children has improved. The corporation has made a continuing commitment to the school. Individuals, businesses, nonprofit organizations, and churches from coast to coast are realizing that each community must reclaim its right to safety by nurturing its youth. It is efforts such as these, along with the dedication of hard-working school personnel, that will turn things around.

We Must Be Determined to Accept Students Who Reject Us

Emotionally scarred and wounded students have learned to hate. Because important others have treated them with abuse or have been unable to nurture, such students develop the view that the world is filled with hostility. Expecting hostility, they act first, and do provocative things to make others angry. Provoked adults often become angry at the student and say or do something to show they're boss. Having made yet another adult feel hostile, the student's world view is confirmed. This "hostility cycle" (see Figure 1.1) will continue uninterrupted until adults who regularly participate in the life of the hostile student understand this dynamic and refuse to play the game. The key attitude is to stay personal with the student without personalizing his or her baggage. For example, when a student like this votes on your assignment with his middle finger, it's okay to say, "Hiram, I know sometimes you feel so angry that you want others to hurt as much as you do, but there are better ways to tell me you hurt than hurting me (personal)." It is less helpful to think, "The little brat has it in for me" (taking it personally).

Children who have been neglected or abused often get trapped in a cycle of further abuse. They love the ones who hurt them and hurt the ones who love them. Sometimes their world is so full of pain that they create less hostile imaginary worlds of their own and cannot tell which is which. They do not see what others see and cannot understand concepts like "truth." When you give them love they may reject or even attack you. Even when we love them with all our heart, they might fail to accept our love. It is hard to continue to care. Yet when we don't give up, many of these children can learn to trust and become healthy, functioning individuals.

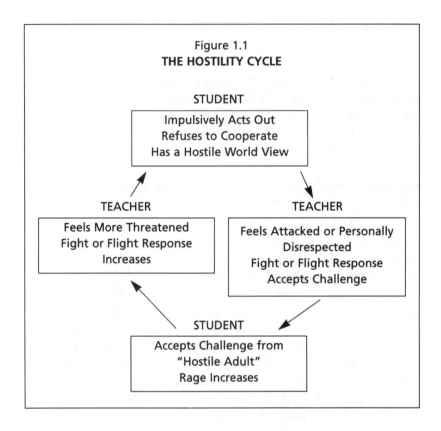

Figure 1.1
THE HOSTILITY CYCLE

We Must Always Treat Students with Dignity

Successful educators convey a basic sense of respect to their students by listening, being open to feedback from them, explaining why they want things done a certain way, and giving them some say in classroom affairs that affect them. They are able to respectfully insist upon decent behavior because they are unafraid of calling attention to unacceptable words or actions without put-downs, sarcasm, scolds, and threats. The message is: You are important, and so am I!! It is difficult to feel dignified when students tell you where to go and how quickly to get there. It is especially difficult when our professionalism is challenged. We can easily become cynical in such a climate, yet nothing exacerbates aggression and hostility faster than a cynical attitude. We must continually resist viewing and responding to troubling students as "worthless ingrates" and, as important, we must help less-experienced colleagues who are filled with vigor and enthusiasm by banning the "you'll see" faculty room chatter.

Reacting with dignity to the very moments in which students are rendering indignities to ourselves and each other sends a very powerful message that shows capability and strength without brutality. The reality is that explosive students will protect their dignity at all costs, some even with their lives. In school, students must know that their dignity will always be maintained.

Violence Prevention Works Best When Integrated with Effective Teaching Practices

One of the primary purposes that bring students and teachers together is the acquisition of knowledge and mastery of academic skills. But processes and procedures of violence prevention, confrontation, and resolution should be a regular component of the curriculum.

Even in the best of circumstances, nonviolent conflicts occur regularly in classrooms and can provide opportunities to teach effective resolution skills within an educational context. Regularly "staging" conflict situations while presenting skills such as active listening or paraphrasing increases the probability that such skills will really be used. There is also no doubt that engaging, interesting, and motivating instruction leaves little room for aggression and hostility to develop or exacerbate.

"Obedience" Has a Place Only in Limited Contexts

When danger or safety are at issue, obedience-based discipline methods are important. However, the main focus of violence prevention is assisting students in developing responsibility. Obedience-based discipline relies heavily upon threats, rewards, and punishments. The challenge is geared toward identifying either adequate rewards or sufficiently noxious punishments. Because there is a heavy reliance upon the use of external methods of control, authorities must always be visible to enforce policy.

Only strong values motivate us to control our naturally violent nature. Before a nonviolent choice can be made, though, an individual needs a potent desire to do so. Students must know in their minds, hearts, and spirits that hurting others is wrong.

There is no doubt that behavior change among hardened, antisocial, and angry students cannot occur simply by offering more love, caring, and opportunities for decision making (all necessary components in developing responsibility). Conventional behavioral methods that are obedience oriented ("do as I say and you will be rewarded or punished if you do not") are occasionally required in the early stages for such youth and those around them to feel a sense of safety and security. But since school is a place of education, its primary focus must be creating responsible decision making among youth who either lack the skill or will to do what is right.

Violence in the Classroom

"On March 6, 1986, I was shot during class by one of my high school freshmen Algebra students. I was very fortunate that the bullet passed in and out without doing any serious damage to me. While I was in the hospital (I was only there two days and two nights), I had many calls from my fellow teachers and other friends and family. Many of them wondered if I would leave the teaching profession. After giving it some thought, I decided I would not give up my job. I was supporting myself, I was trained to teach, and I felt that I wanted to continue teaching. I was determined that what happened to me was not going to affect the rest of my life.

...Was it easy to go back? No. Because when I did return (about 2 ½ weeks after the shooting) someone put a threatening note on my desk. Since there was no way for the school or police to determine who sent the note, it was mutually agreed that it might be best if I remained out of school for the rest of the school year and returned in September. I also transferred to another school in the district. (There are three high schools in this district).

...It has now been seven years since the incident. I still occasionally hear references to it from the students, but for the most part it has died down. The first two years were very bad but that is all in the past. When something like this occurs in a school, it affects the entire staff. It was, of course, worse for me because I was the one directly involved. But as I said earlier, many of the teachers now wonder if it will happen to them. This was not an inner city school or one where you might expect some violence. But as we have seen in the last few years, there is more and more of this in schools all over the country -- not just the inner city."

—A Teacher in Indiana

We Can't Always Treat Everyone the Same

In our *Discipline with Dignity* training, this concept often arouses controversy. Since so many educators were trained to believe that good discipline requires a consistent approach, many schools persist in standardizing disciplinary procedures that can be applied to everyone based upon what they do and how often they do it. In practice, there are always more complex circumstances, and many initiatives fail because those areas weren't factored into the overall picture. For example, some schools with a zero tolerance policy on student aggression have felt compelled to call the police about a kindergarten student biting the teacher. Although there may be an occasional educator who might view this as good and necessary, most thoughtful adults would agree that this constitutes overkill bordering on the bizarre. We advocate creating clear rules that are predicated upon a set of values that are taught to students. When violations of the rules occur, educators need a range of available consequences that can be implemented to teach the students more responsible behavior.

Consistency has more to do with holding students accountable to limits (rules) and does not equate to "zero tolerance." Effective programs have a variety of consequences that help the student learn new behaviors and reduce the old. Zero tolerance means treating everyone the same, and that is one of the greatest causes of hostility and aggression.

Those who can no longer tolerate the throwing away of young lives through illogical and damaging policies have shared many horrible tales of how zero tolerance shatters lives. One example is from a middle school that had a zero tolerance weapons rule. Any student who brought a weapon to school was sent to the office, a parent was required to come to school to claim the weapon, and the student received a suspension. This was applied in every case of a weapon brought to school: no exceptions, no excuses. And it worked for nearly every case, but nearly doesn't mean all. One day a young girl was found with seven large knives in her backpack. She was sent to the office, and her mother was called in and given the knives. The girl received a long-term suspension and the police were called.

While waiting for the police to arrive, the girl broke down and through her tears revealed that she feared for her mother's life because the night before the mother had attempted suicide by cutting herself with a knife. The daughter, not knowing what else to do, brought every knife she could find to school to save her mother.

How unfortunate that the knives were returned to the mother and the girl was punished. If only this girl could have shared her fear with a school counselor or called a hotline or hid the knives somewhere else. But to penalize her for trying to save her mother because of an inflexible policy runs counter to all that we have learned from students and common sense about violence prevention.

Educators Must Take Good Emotional Care of Themselves

Too few noneducation professionals truly appreciate the incredible outflow of energy, dedication, and commitment required to make the difference in the lives of students who come from problematic, dysfunctional environments. To keep yourself from burning out, take good emotional care of yourself.

Students who are difficult, disruptive, or dangerous evoke fear and anger. Recognize these feelings, and create a system of support for yourself. Take a short walk during lunch or preparation time during school. Talk to a trusted colleague about what you feel, or talk to a colleague about a subject other than school. Take a sick day once or twice a year and do something fun. This is just as legitimate as a sick day when you have the flu. Do all that you can to stay physically and emotionally healthy. You will be a more effective and helpful teacher if you feel fit in every way.

Choosing a Different Path

Although aggression is a natural part of being human, the lack of caring and lack of remorse about violence today is more serious than ever before. We believe one of the major contributing factors to this is a gradual change from teaching values to simply rewarding and punishing children. Until students understand that it is wrong to hurt, they will not change their behavior. If the family has failed to convey this, other institutions must do what they can to return us to a culture of values and principles. To that end, religion can teach religious values to those who will listen. Businesses can treat customers with respect and dignity. Youth groups can teach a variety of values to children. The school, too, has responsibility to teach values.

Violence in the Community

"Many Americans view rural midwestern towns like Rapid City, South Dakota, as crime-free. I wish that were so. Many are fleeing from urban cities and moving to the rural towns hoping to escape the violence. It is true we do not have the bigger crime issues of the larger cities but unfortunately violence is a rapidly growing problem here.

In Rapid City we have seen an alarming increase in juvenile crime during the past five years and gangs have started showing up. Twenty years ago no one locked their house or took their keys out of their car and you could walk anywhere feeling safe. Now we do not. Many people complain that there is a growing lack of respect for people and property. National statistics reflect crime in rural towns is now at the level that urban cities experienced in 1966 when Congress decided to declare a 'war on crime.'

Recently our newly formed Rapid City Community Coalition for Violence Prevention took this warning seriously and initiated a community safety survey. Of those individuals responding to the survey, 80 percent felt safe but 77 percent felt violence was an increasing problem in Rapid City. More than 25 percent (350 people) responded by writing their names on the survey saying they were willing to get involved.

We started a community grassroots movement called S.A.V.E. Rapid City (Stand Against a Violent Environment). Our mission is to empower the community to reclaim our neighborhoods from violence, restoring them as safe places to live and raise families. We are training individuals in neighborhoods to help facilitate dialogue and discussion about violence, how it is affecting them, root causes, and possible solutions. We are helping the community to redefine violence from the traditional ideas of crimes (hitting, stabbing, murdering, etc.) to violence meaning any word, look, sign, or act that hurts a person's body or feelings. By redefining violence to include behaviors like name calling, rumors, etc., prevention can start at an earlier stage. "

—Pamela Teaney Thomas
Rapid City School District
Rapid City, South Dakota

We need to transform every school into a community that actively demonstrates, models, and advocates a commitment to humanity. *All life is precious and needs to be respected, protected, and valued.* We fear not an overexposure to positive values but the damage done when the entire realm of values is claimed as the exclusive property of any one group. Educational values that relate to cooperation, safety, racism, learning, altruism, and remorse must be taught and reinforced at school. We will not survive as a culture unless they are.

When students see the proper commitment, modeling, and instruction, they can and will make the school a better place. For example, a school district outside of Chicago encouraged its students to be involved in reducing violence. The children filled the halls with antiviolence posters, put on an assembly about violence prevention, and invented a slogan to say when tensions mounted: It's okay to walk away.

We do not simply wish to teach children to rise above their impulses, drives, and emotions. We want to teach them to reach out and aspire to a higher dimension, one inhabited by values, a strong sense of what is right as well as what is wrong, and an understanding and belief in the essential sanctity of the human spirit.

It is clear that to be human is to live with a built-in predisposition to violent behavior. Whether we ignore it, lean towards it, or relish it, we cannot escape it. Nor can we escape its personal and social consequences. However, the fact that being human means we must face violence does not mean we have to act violently. We can learn to act differently—and we can teach children that they have those choices, too.

2

The Importance of Values and Principles

We cannot end violence by . . .
Using or developing technology
Building walls
Marginalizing groups or individuals
Thinking of newer, harsher rules and punishments.
Ignoring it
Giving up
Avoiding values

I am angry at you, and I want to hurt you. What will stop me? What stops you from hurting others when you are angry?

Is it fear of getting caught and the resulting consequences? If so, which deters you more: what might happen to you, how you feel about yourself (guilt or shame), or the possibility of disappointing loved ones? Will you be deterred by knowing other, more acceptable, ways to express your anger? Or will you be deterred by receiving psychological help from a trained specialist?

All of these possibilities work from time to time and form the basic components of any violence prevention program. But more is needed. Values are at the core of all decision making. Without teaching the simple value that hurting others is wrong, we cannot expect anything we do to make a long-term difference.

There is no way to ever stop someone from hurting another person if that is what he or she really wants. This is true in the workplace, on the street, on public transportation, or in school. The first and most significant step in ending violence is to stop people from wanting to hurt others, and values are the best way to achieve this. At their core, schools must honor and teach the idea that humans are precious and never should be hurt.

Although some believe that rewards and punishments are sufficient for teaching core values, we firmly disagree. We won't go over this debate, which has been written about in far more detail than we endeavor to do here (Molnar and Lindquist 1989, Wlodkowski and Jaynes 1990, Curwin 1992, Kohn 1993). But let us point out that rewards teach children that if they do good, they will receive something in return. They learn that values can be bargained for, can be exchanged, and, in a very broad sense, have commercial worth. Punishments teach that it is bad to get caught, and they encourage excuse making, sneakiness, and covering your tracks.

Both rewards and punishments fail the following critical test: How do they influence behavior when no one is watching? Basically, they have no influence whatsoever. We do not believe success has been achieved if a teacher yells at a student for hitting; the student never strikes out again in the classroom; but the student hits on the playground, in the parking lot, in the lunchroom, or on the bus. Rewards and punishments teach obedience only. Values and consequences teach responsibility.

As Tough as Necessary

The concept of being "as tough as necessary" came to realization through our struggles with the concept of zero tolerance. Both of us agreed that zero tolerance sends a powerful message to the school community that violent, aggressive behavior will not be tolerated. We also acknowledged that the message was ambiguous, with at least two different and apparently opposite meanings, and that it was a simplistic way for educators to avoid responsibility by irrationally dealing with all misbehavior in the same way. Zero tolerance in effect says to students, "We will not listen to you." At the same time, it shouts, "Violence will not be tolerated! If you want to stay here, you will not hurt others."

Once we could clearly recognize the merits as well as the weaknesses in the diverging points of view, we were able to invent a new concept that combined the strengths of each view and mostly eliminated the problems. "As tough as necessary" finds the harmony between the seemingly opposite positions. This new synthesis sends the message that violence will not be tolerated, and yet we will not deal with students in cookie-cutter fashion. We can meet their needs without resorting to formulas and still protect the school and its inhabitants from unacceptable behavior. Further, we trust ourselves as professionals more than we trust formulas to be caretakers of youngsters.

It is readily apparent that "as tough as necessary" is far superior to zero tolerance if we examine each policy by how it teaches children to behave. Would anyone want a school board or superintendent who had a zero tolerance attitude when dealing with teachers? Do you know anyone who was raised by a zero tolerant parent? What might they say about how that affected their childhood? Could a marriage survive a zero tolerance spouse? More important, do we want children to have zero tolerance, particularly when they are angry?

There is no contention over the need for clear, firm limits; certain behaviors are not tolerable. "As tough as necessary" allows us to honor and enforce those limits without modeling zero tolerance. We would much rather see children who are as tough as necessary rather than ones who are zero tolerant.

The process of creating a school that values nonviolent expressions of aggression and confronts hostile attitudes and behaviors encompasses four stages:

- Identify the core values of the school.
- Create rules and consequences using these values.
- Model the values during interactions with students and staff.
- Eliminate interventions that violate the core values.

Identify the Core Values of the School

All communities share core values that bond them for whatever reason they come together. Some values are shared by nearly all: Killing is wrong. Other values are shared by most community members: Hard work is good. Some values are shared by a few: The ballet is worth funding. A community holds together—be it a country, a family, a corporation, or a school—as long as enough common values are shared to create cohesiveness and a collective sense of purpose.

All who are part of a school community agree on certain values: School is a place where people learn. Another value might be: This school will be safe. As principles and values become more specific, they are more likely to generate disagreement. For example: In this school we will use consequences, not punishments. Or: Discipline is part of every teacher's responsibility.

Most faculties and staffs, and especially students, do not know the stated values of a school, which often are cloaked in mission statements or 10-year plans on file with the superintendent or school board. Thus, the starting point for violence prevention is articulating and agreeing on values and principles.

Beginning with the faculty and eventually including staff, students, and parents, develop a list of core values related to violence, aggression, and hostility. These values should include statements of beliefs or principles that speak to the way individuals or groups in the school treat each other. Following is a list of core values to use as a starting point. Keep in mind that the best values come from the people in your own school, and all groups need a say in what the values will be.

- School is a place where people feel safe so that we don't hurt others on the inside or the outside.
- School is a place where we learn that we are responsible for what we do.
- School is a place where everyone has equal worth—and lots of it.
- School is a place where we learn that my way is not the only way.
- School is a place where we protect and look out for one another, rather than hurt or attack one another.
- School is a place where doing little things to help can make big differences.
- School is a place were we solve our problems peacefully.

Voices on Violence

"... violence will always be a part of life. No matter how hard you try to stop it, it will still be around. If I had a reason to commit a violent act, then I would. ...If violence can solve a problem, then it should be used as a problem solver. Everyone should do what they feel is right. I feel that if the law can act violently, then why can't citizens do the same?"

— A male student

There are many ways to help people in the school develop core values, from simply informing faculty of the values listed in the school's mission statement to beginning from scratch and creating a new list with focus groups from different school populations. When developing core values, the following points are important:

- **Ignoring this phase of the process—or doing it at the end—will significantly reduce the potential success of the program.** The more hostile your school environment and the more aggressive students' behavior, the more critical this phase is to reducing violence. Violence reduction *begins* with values.

- **As the list of values or principles becomes more specific, they are likely to generate more disagreement.** This is natural and should not be discouraged. Below you will see how such conflict can be used in a way that eventually can strengthen the school.

- **All rules in the school will be subjected to the values test.** If any rule violates or compromises any of the values, *the rule* must be modified or removed. No rule can require behavior that is contrary to antiviolence values.

- **All consequences in the school will be subjected to the values test.** Any consequence that violates or compromises any of the values must be modified or removed.

- **All of the people in the school—including administrators, teachers, aides, and students—will be held accountable to live by these values and to model them.**

• These values will be taught to students as part of the school orientation, as part of the instructional process, and after rules are broken.

Resolving Values Conflicts Among Faculty and Staff

One of the most difficult tasks we have ever undertaken was trying to get the faculty of a medium-sized middle school to agree on how to resolve their disagreement over what to do about a fight between two boys. Derrick, the 8th grade bully, saw Jose in the hall talking with four or five other students. Derrick approached Jose and began calling him names, shoving him, and threatening to do him greater harm. Jose backed off and tried to joke about the situation, but Derrick shoved him again. Then Derrick threw a punch, and Jose hit back. Mrs. Samuelson, who saw the event from the beginning, hauled both boys to the office. The principal suspended both boys for one day, explaining that further action would be taken once the facts were examined.

The principal discussed the incident with the staff at their regular staff meeting later that afternoon. There were two clear positions that polarized the school: (1) The school rule was a zero tolerance, no fight rule: automatic one-week suspension for both parties. (2) One boy initiated the fight while the other tried to defuse the situation, and then defended himself when attacked.

After hours of heated disagreement and occasional personal exchanges, something unexpected happened. By listening to the various needs, positions, and values, two teachers synthesized a new way of organizing the information that met everyone's goals. The solution exemplifies the quality of the "as tough as necessary" model. Derrick received a week suspension with the additional requirement of meeting with a counselor to find other ways to show his "leadership" qualities. Eventually Derrick became responsible for preventing hallway fights. He took his assignment seriously because it gave him the opportunity to meet one of his basic needs in an altruistic manner.

Jose received no additional suspension, but he did learn other techniques for dealing with bullies.

The school also tried to enlist student support in promoting an "It's okay to walk away" campaign, which has thus far met with only moderate success.

Voices on Violence

"I may be a child but I do know something about life. I know that anger, that causes violence, not only can be caused by a parents style of raising but also by an older brother or sister. I myself have an older brother. He is 16. He hits me when he is angry. Often I can't tell what upsets him but something does."

— A female student

We wish to focus on how the staff resolved their heartfelt differences in developing such an insightful and creative solution. To their credit, they stayed educational rather than falling into the trap of politics. They achieved this rare feat by focusing on the good of the children they were there to serve, rather than worrying about who would win the argument. Credit must be shared by the principal, whose leadership lifted the debate to what really mattered, and the staff, who recognized the need to resolve the matter professionally.

All schools can benefit from a healthy debate about values with the goal of understanding and developing more advanced, sophisticated techniques. It is not always possible to discover harmonious synthesis between contradictory values, but at the very least, faculty members need to hear and understand each other.

Resolving values conflicts is an essential part of organizing new concepts and involving the whole faculty in the resulting product. A word of caution: avoid voting, straw voting or attempts at consensus selection prematurely. Give the process time enough for all to share what they really believe and to hear what matters to others.

We suggest organizing each conflict according to the following scheme: belief, values, and challenges. Consider the following examples of various violence-related beliefs.

Belief: There is no absolute way to stop anyone who wants to hurt another person.

Value: No one has the right to hurt others. No one deserves to be hurt.

Challenge: The only long-term solution is to discover ways to stop children from wanting to hurt others. Creating rules and firm boundaries is necessary to establishing limits, to demonstrate that violent behavior will not be tolerated, and to teach right from wrong. Yet these boundaries often become barriers to frequent rule violators who feel walled out, especially if they are ostracized or marginalized in the process. For some, these conditions encourage them to strike back without remorse. Each school must determine how to establish strong barriers and boundaries that keep potentially violent students in rather than push them out.

Belief: Safety is necessary for learning to occur.

Value: All children have a right to feel and be safe in school.

Challenge: Safety is expensive, both financially and in terms of the rights we sacrifice. It's accompanied by a loss of freedom. The safer we become, the less democracy we have. Many U.S. citizens are willing to sacrifice their Constitutional rights to feel safer, as demonstrated by a Presidential order for a sweep of guns in a low-income housing project in Chicago. President Clinton ordered a sweep of apartments to answer the fear expressed by its residents. The action was later halted by the Supreme Court as a violation of the Fourth Amendment. Are weapons so much of a threat that we need to sacrifice protection from illegal search and seizure?

Not enough emphasis on safety has obvious consequences. However, more subtle are the consequences from giving up too much freedom, which may actually increase violence. The Oklahoma City bombing appears to have been committed in the name of freedom by irrational people who feared the government was taking liberty and basic rights away. Militias are another manifestation of people fed up with government interference, even for their own protection. Determining the best balance between safety and life in a democratic society is one of our great challenges. It is one that every school must face with rigorous and thoughtful dialogue.

Belief: Political attitudes drive school decision making.

Value: Educational decisions are best made for the good of children, not to advance a political agenda.

Challenge: If any antiviolence school reform is to work, it must appear to be reasonable to most citizens from all spectrums of the political arena without alienating anyone's sense of decency. This means achieving a goal that has rarely, if ever, been accomplished: leave politics out of the school decision-making process.

Schools have a right and a responsibility to teach values: not religious values, not family values, but educational and community values. These values relate to cooperation, safety, racism, learning, and altruism. Children do not commit violent acts because they have learned too many positive values, nor do they behave violently because they developed values on their own. Examples of educational values are:

- School is a place where people learn.
- Students should be safe at all times.
- Cooperation is preferred to conflict.
- Everyone is responsible to help others.
- Racism, bigotry, sexism, and "anti" any group are not welcome.

Students, too, need a say in the values and principles of the school (Curwin and Mendler 1988, Curwin 1992, Mendler 1992). The more involved students are in developing the principles and values upon which rules based, the more likely they are to follow them. In addition, violence prevention depends on students valuing nonviolent behavior. Obviously, the more involved students are in creating the values, the more likely they are to respond with alternative behavior when they feel aggressive.

No less than once every four years—and preferably more often—each school should ask students what values they want to represent their school. The processes used to generate this list might include using all English classes or homerooms to brainstorm initial lists. Or use focus groups or student government. Once master lists have been generated, return to smaller groups for discussion, debate, and selection of a final list. Student-generated values will likely be similar or identical to faculty lists. Although faculty and students often have different views, different needs, and very different demands relating to many school issues, these differences often dissipate when it comes to safety. All need and want to feel safe, secure, appreciated, needed, competent, and reinforced. All need to feel that they belong, that they are welcomed.

Create Rules and Consequences Using the Core Values

Those who use the *Discipline with Dignity* approach report that one of its greatest strengths is an emphasis on values rather than deterrents. Responsibility is the program's paramount goal, and teaching students to base their decisions on values is at the heart of nurturing responsible behavior.

In the framework for teaching responsibility and for handling rule violations, which we call a social contract, all rules are based on principles. We have found that most schools misinterpret the adage "Have few rules, two or three" by substituting principles for rules. Instead of using a behavioral rule such as, "Keep your hands and feet to yourselves," a much more general principle is used: "Be nice." The problem is that nice really has no specific meaning, so 20 or 30 rules get generated about everything from hitting to saying please. Often, these real rules are never stated and are enforced at the teacher's whim.

This confusion of rules and principles is self-defeating. Rules work when they set clear limits and are stated in behavioral terms. We all know that there are thousands of things we should or should not do. Administrators or teachers must pick out those four or five rules that they want to establish as priorities to avoid and control violence.

We solve this dilemma by starting with principles, based on values, and developing clear, behavioral rules from them. We limit the number of rules by eliminating unnecessary ones, not by hiding them under catch-all generalities. Let's look at the values stated earlier in this chapter and see an example of a rule for each.

These rules are examples. Each school or classroom can develop principles and rules with the help of students to meet particular needs and problems. Principles and rules work together because values motivate and rules set limits. Sell the principles; enforce the rules.

When rules are broken, they must be enforced, and the principle behind them must be explained, taught, clarified, and modeled. As important as this is for social contracts, it is more so for controlling aggression and violence. There is no alternative to teaching values as the core of violence prevention.

Model Values with Students and Staff Members

A startling sight in a school office offered us one of the best illustrations for the necessity of modeling. While slapping her son in the face, a mother shouted, "And who taught you to hit?"

Value	Rule
• School is a place where people feel safe so that we don't hurt others on the inside or the outside.	• No weapons allowed in school.
• School is a place where we learn that we are responsible for what we do.	• Hand in your schoolwork on time.
• School is a place where every one has equal worth—and lots of it.	• Do not interrupt others when they are speaking.
• School is a place where we learn that my way is not the only way.	• Settle disagreements with words, not fists.
• School is a place where we protect and look out for one another, rather than hurt or attack one another.	• No put-downs allowed.
• School is a place where doing little things to help can make big differences.	• Tell others to cool it when you see them wanting to fight.
• School is a place where we solve our problems peacefully.	• Keep your hands and feet to yourselves.

Being a positive role model is often difficult, especially when anger and frustration displace reason. However, modeling is an essential element in teaching children how to express their emotions nonviolently. How we resolve conflicts with students illustrates what we believe far better than what we say about acceptable behavior. It is easy to tell children to walk away from a personal put-down on the playground. It is difficult for us to walk away when a student puts us down in the classroom.

We are overwhelmed with examples of negative role models. We once admired government leaders, business executives, athletes, clergy, police, and even lawyers. Times have changed. When the number of positive role models decreases, those who remain are more precious than ever. If we tell children we won't tolerate anger and frustration—and then respond to certain situations with those very feelings—how will youngsters learn anything different?

Children do not learn alternatives to physically or emotionally hurting others when important adults react to their mistakes, immaturity, or misjudgments in humiliating ways. By asking ourselves how we want our children to respond to other children who taunt them, interfere with their lives, or otherwise harass them, we discover a framework for our own interactions with students. Often, we ourselves have trouble staying within that framework in real situations where our own emotions spark an attack response.

By examining this imperfection within ourselves, we can understand why emotional expression is so difficult for children. We can best help them to overcome this problem by overcoming it ourselves. In large part, our ability to teach children nonviolent responses depends on how successful we are in changing our own responses when interacting with them.

Modeling Values During Conflict Situations

It is far more meaningful to behave consistently with our values than to lecture about them. Children watch us more carefully and internalize what we do more than we ever realize. A school and the individuals who work there need to look closely at their values and behaviors to see where they can improve the congruence between the two. If it is too difficult for the faculty to live with certain values, then in all likelihood the values will be difficult for children.

The most important modeling for violence prevention is for faculty and staff to demonstrate anger control and conflict resolution with students when they are in actual situations that test them. How do you want students to respond on the playground or parking lot when a student says, "You suck!"? The way you intervene to head off possible violence between two students or the way you react if an epithet is directed at you will show students a response that is firm, indicates that insults or escalation to violence is unacceptable, but does not provoke violence.

A helpful strategy (for individuals or in a staff meeting) is to write on paper how you want students to express their anger toward you and how they should resolve classroom conflicts with you and other students. Then teach your students these techniques and, most importantly, use them yourself when you are in situations that demand them.

Voices on Violence

"Me and about three other people were down at the beach walking around shooting bottle rockets, we had been drinking that night. We seen some fip's sitting around a bonfire so we got on top of a dune and started throwing bottle rockets at them, all the people were freaking out we headed back up to my friends house and got away safely. The reason why we did it is because, we didn't have anything better to do plus we were just drunk."

—A male student

Administrators can include in the evaluation process how effectively teachers and staff actually behave with students and how they teach students in accordance with the agreed-upon values. The goal is not to force these values on anyone but to make them a genuine part of the school culture. These values are serious and must be treated as such. It subverts all of the school's efforts to decrease student violence if a significant number of those who work there ignore what you teach your students and model behavior inconsistent with what you want students to incorporate as their own.

In the same way, faculty and staff can be encouraged to treat each other by the same values and rules when they interact. Administrators can be encouraged to model their interactions with other professionals, especially anger, in the same way they want those professionals to treat children. In our experience working with teachers, we hear a common request: "If we are expected to treat students with dignity, then we want to be treated with dignity by our administration." When everyone in the school behaves consistently with the stated and agreed upon values, students are given both subtle and explicit instruction for how to behave. We create the best chance for students to behave appropriately when we nurture a school culture that defines violence and hostility as unacceptable outlets for aggression and where children see most adults behaving and succeeding accordingly.

Modeling Values During Instruction

There are two ways to use values in the instructional process: by using curriculum to illustrate nonviolent values and by treating students with dignity as they struggle through the difficulty of learning.

Examples of the former abound. In English or reading classes, thousands of selections raise questions about violent behavior and suggest alternatives to aggression. Social studies offers examples throughout history and contemporary life in every unit and lesson. In science, students can consider whether we should have developed the nuclear bomb. Are scientists responsible for what happens to society when advanced weapons are developed? Are there implications for violence, either positive or negative, with the increase in use of computers and the Internet?

We do not think it is necessary to make a forced fit between content and core values. Not every lesson or subject is appropriate. There are enough subjects where antiviolence values are the natural lesson without the need for any major manipulation.

Some will wonder about the issue of whether rewards and punishments should be substituted for values-based motivation and incentives for learning. It is easy to fall into the trap of rewards and punishments as instructional tools because of their speed and ease of use. With all the other responsibilities teachers have and the number of students who do not wish to learn, it is understandable why some teachers settle for quick-fix instructional tools. However, in the long term, these methods actually make it harder for students to learn, and they demonstrate that we do not believe in our own stated values. We never want to tell students by our actions that it is okay to compromise values for expediency. That is the same rationalization they use for hitting rather than discussing.

Some believe that treating students with dignity means rewarding good behavior. True dignity is based not on external rewards, but rather on the genuine belief that each student has worth. Rather than simply reward those students who score high, resolve to encourage and respect all those who struggle to learn, realizing that what is most worth learning is often the most difficult to learn. Dignity, if it is to have worth, must never be cheapened.

Eliminate Interventions That Violate Core Values

In the same way that children learn from us, we have learned from our past experiences. The way we were treated as children still influences our choices as adults. Unfortunately, when we rely primarily on our own personal experiences to select strategies and methods for dealing with children who live in today's world, we miss the larger picture of how today's children interpret our messages. We must consider ways of treating students that at one time might have been potentially effective but now cause more harm than good. Each violates the basic core values discussed above.

Corporal Punishment

Corporal punishment is restricted or banned in most states. In the states that allow corporal punishment, many districts do not use or permit it. We strongly urge administrators, teachers, and parents who still believe that corporal punishment is effective to find and use other methods. We must constantly remain vigilant against the forces who will try to re-introduce corporal punishment as a legitimate form of discipline. Vocal minorities have disproportionate influence on schools and laws. While our goal is to make corporal punishment illegal in all states, we must also work to insure that other states don't move in the opposite direction.

Hitting children teaches them the values of force, degradation, disrespect, and humiliation. These have nothing to do with the values of cooperation, respect, love, communication, and learning. Children have a right to learn to behave without being abused in any way. Schools should not give in to simplistic demands for corporal punishment even when parents spank or request that schools do likewise.

We frequently ask participants at our seminars and training sessions to identify if they were spanked as children and believed that they turned out okay. Usually, several participants raise their hands affirmatively because many, if not most, adults were spanked at one time or another as they grew up. Yet our memories are not reliable interpreters of childhood events. How can anyone know for sure whether spanking helped or hurt his or her overall development? In days past, no one talked about child abuse, so spanking's image was rarely tarnished.

More to the point are the changes in the basic family structure over the last few decades. Spankings used to be given in the context of pointed lectures. Children would sit with mom or dad and hear stories with morals. They would learn values from grandparents, parents, or religious leaders, and they could feel secure as part of a greater whole. Spankings were a small part of something big called "family."

Now when children are spanked, it's a big part of something a lot smaller. Without everyday values lessons in a variety of contexts, spankings only teach that force is good and hitting is legitimate. When children come from homes where being hit is routine, it is especially irrational and destructive to use corporal punishment in school. These children must learn other methods of control and alternative expressions of anger.

Threats

Threats work when they are limited to specific dangerous situations that require an immediate response: stopping a toddler from crossing a busy street, telling a child to put down a knife, stopping a fight that is about to erupt. But threats have no long-term value, and usually they prompt countermeasures that raise the stakes.

Many educators who see the short-term value of threats honestly believe they work because fear changes behavior so quickly. But in reality, the long-term results of threats are worsened behavior, deteriorated trust and communication, and potential for a violent incident to occur. Nobody can threaten a student into having positive values or behaving appropriately.

When initial threats fail, more severe threats are issued. All of us who work with or raise children have found ourselves in our own self-made, threat-based traps. We eventually issue ultimatums that are so severe we don't want to actually carry them out. If the child still resists, we realize we can't go through with the threat, so we threaten even more severely, praying that the child finally gives in so we don't have to do something we can't tolerate or teach the child that we don't follow through. All the while, the child is learning an "adult" way to get what you want.

How many school fights begin with a small threat that escalated when a counterthreat was issued? Many children have told us that it is better to be hurt or to hurt others than it is to back down. If children can learn alternatives to threats or techniques for diffusing them before it becomes too late, a great deal of violence could be avoided.

Intimidating Students

We once met a young woman named Roxanne. She was 14-years-old with orange hair, numerous tattoos, and rings in her ears, nose, lips, and various other parts of her body. She also had a 29-year-old gangbanger boyfriend and a police record. She told us she had no fear of detention, suspensions, or calls to her home. These threats were often promised—and occasionally carried out—without any effect on her behavior. She reacted to the school's threats by both threatening and intimidating those who "got in her face."

Maybe the school could get rid of Roxanne, but the school cannot get rid of all who refuse to be model students. And even if the school does remove students like Roxanne from campus, they cannot be removed from society.

Intimidation works with nice middle-class kids who are nonviolent, generally stay out of trouble, and have no behavior problems. But pushing a student "against the wall" does not work with children whose everyday lives are worse than anything with which you can threaten them. It does not work with victims of violence or abuse. It does not work for students who have gone through the court system or who have lived in juvenile homes. It does not work for students who do not fear you but whom you fear.

Using a Student as an Example for Others

The most common reason given for public discipline is that other students must see that rule violators are punished so others will be deterred from breaking rules themselves. In fact, this only creates humiliation for the rule violator and the need to restore dignity, thus sparking an escalating power struggle.

Over the years, *Discipline with Dignity* has proved that discipline is best done privately. When a student is used as an example, the hidden message is that it is okay to sacrifice the dignity of one student to teach lessons to the others. Yet violence reduction depends on the core value that no one can be hurt. While consequences for rule violations are necessary, the primary goal of interventions with rule breakers is to teach better, more responsible behavior. Hurtful responses to violators validates the use of violence by others with different goals.

All hope of decreasing violent behavior depends on teaching and modeling positive, nonviolent values. All the rules, consequences, or punishments in the world, with all the pseudo-toughness of a zero-tol-erance attitude, will do nothing more than add to the explosive mix of a rapidly changing world. We start with values and principles—not merely inculcating students to believe without thinking, but modeling, teaching, and providing choices. By developing a set of nonviolent val-ues and by ensuring with diligence that the policies, procedures, and practices of the school are aligned with them, we can help students begin to learn to treat others in less violent ways.

3

Strategies for the Teacher

Students cannot stop hurting others
until they stop hurting themselves.
Students cannot begin to care about others
until they begin to care about themselves.

If you grew up in a neighborhood with a strong sense of community before or during the 1950s, perhaps this story sounds familiar to you. When you walked to school each morning, you knew you would pass your friend's father waiting for the bus to go to work. Occasionally you would see another friend's mother peeking out of her window, checking out the people on the street. Yet another mother would wave hello and tell you to have a nice day. These people knew you, and you knew them. They made you feel protected and safe.

When you felt like misbehaving, you knew you'd better be careful because someone who knew you probably would find out and either deal with you directly or, more likely, tell your parents. You weren't so much afraid that you would be punished, although that might happen. More devastating was that your parents would be disappointed in you.

That was one of the strongest deterrents to misbehaving.

This sense of community, as well this sense of values, is no longer a reality for many young people. It is common for many to be unaware of who lives next door. Ironically, it seems that in the last few years, we've increasingly heard that "it takes a village" to raise a child. The First Lady of the United States, Hillary Clinton, even used the phrase as the title for a 1996 book. Although the phrase has become trite, it is true that the community influences the child.

While much attention is correctly focused on the absence of family values as a cause for many of today's problems, lack of community support is also a serious factor. In past years, a child from a dysfunctional family had a good chance of being mentored by a caring adult from his or her community: a friend's parent, scout leader, religious leader, or teacher. Some children still have this experience, but not many.

Educators need to create classroom and school communities that establish accountability for student behavior in a nurturing, caring context. Schools are communities in and of themselves, and they can model values, just as individual teachers do. In schools committed to reducing violence, the community can and does make significant positive differences.

We have found that the development of responsible, thoughtful behavior in children is directly connected to dominant messages that they receive telling them they are respected, understood, and accepted. Stanley Coopersmith's (1967, 1975) work in self-esteem provides a good model for approaches, techniques, and strategies needed to work with today's youth so they make healthy choices that get them what they need while staying safe from the violence that too often results from unexpressed aggression.

Coopersmith found that students with high self-esteem had three factors in their family backgrounds that distinguished them from others: family warmth, clearly defined limits, and a democratic atmosphere that encourages children to learn and practice decision making and problem-solving skills.

These factors influence children in the school as well as the home. Our observations and research tell us that the continuous presence of these characteristics in classrooms is significant in helping students make positive choices. It also is essential that students experience real conflict in controlled settings so that they improve their skills at both recognizing and resolving conflict. Our fourth guideline, recognizing and resolving conflict, acknowledges that need by explaining how conflict between educators and their students provides opportunities for students to witness effective nonviolent ways to defuse possible power struggles that they might use when faced with similar conflict. When discussing this fourth factor, we show educators how to effectively defuse power struggles with individual students and how to handle group misbehavior.

These four factors form the basis of a classroom and school structure designed to promote nonviolence: warmth, clearly defined limits, a democratic atmosphere, and recognizing and resolving conflict. Students who come to school without respect for themselves or others, who have not learned to share, and who have little appreciation for values like courtesy and responsibility need to learn them from adults who care. We must rethink our schools and how they can express themselves in a more family-like way. The recent Carnegie Report's (1996) recommendations that high schools limit size to 600 students, allow teachers only 90 students, and pair each student with an "adult advocate" seems congruent with this concept. That is how you build an intimate, family-like culture in a school.

Although few educators would argue the need for personalizing the learning environment, budget limitations make it difficult to see how achieving these outcomes is possible in the near future. However, if we are serious about connecting with kids before they become violent and teaching them better alternatives after an incidence of violence, then each school and every individual educator needs to accept the challenge of identifying and implementing practices that make kids see school as an affirming, competence-building place. This chapter identifies those practices within the context of four factors.

Warmth

Warmth is one of those elusive concepts that is hard to define with words but easy to recognize when it is present. For students, warmth can best be described in terms of the school being a place where they are respected and loved. Who they are is valued more than what they know. Warmth exists when the development of policies and practices is guided by the question, "How will this improve students' lives?"

At a recent seminar at a suburban high school, a 23-year veteran teacher challenged the idea of his school becoming more student centered. He said, "This school belongs to us (the teachers), because we'll be here long after they (the students) leave. They are visitors here for a few years, and then they are gone. They need to conform to our expectations." Although this colleague's skills and talents are important, he misses the core issue. Without him, the school would continue to exist. Without students, it would not!

We must remember that school is for all children, including those we find unattractive, those who misbehave, and those who don't give it their best. It is our professional duty to welcome and teach them with enthusiasm, care, and courage. To do less diminishes ourselves and all of society.

Without doubt, it takes a deep commitment to fight the temptation to turn away and not engage those students who seem unpredictable, weird, or aggressive towards themselves or others. A friend recently related an incident where she saw a boy in the hall of her high school banging his head repetitively against a locker. Two nearby teachers pretended not to see this worrisome moment. They were understandably afraid and uncertain.

Having been trained to work with difficult youth, my friend approached the boy, got close to him, and told him, "Wow, how terrible the day must be for you. But you can stop hurting yourself now, and then we'll start figuring out what to do next." When she reached out her hand to his, he stopped, acknowledging his inner turmoil. Later, when she asked one of her colleagues why he simply walked past the boy, she was at first told, "The kid is crazy, and that isn't my job!" The same colleague later confessed to being scared.

It is important that we confront our fears and, when necessary, develop the skills that help us know what to do in difficult situations. When I first began working at a facility with juvenile delinquents who were incarcerated for having committed crimes, some violent, a part of me felt terrified. There were times I met one-on-one with a youth in a secured room with nobody else around. I found myself doing things to befriend the residents, ostensibly to develop rapport in my role as a psychologist. That was, of course, necessary and okay, but I could feel and hear the voice of fear from within motivating each of my moves. I was essentially unable to engage the children's fears and anxieties because I was afraid that they might lose control and hurt me. It was only when I confronted myself honestly, and took some self-defense training that I never needed to use, that I felt confident to really be myself and reach out without fear.

When we are afraid of our students, it takes courage to acknowledge the fear and then develop a plan that increases self-confidence. Violent students need confident teachers who know what to do when control is at issue. It is when this confidence is in place that our strategies of "warmth" are especially effective.

With so many students lonely and hurting for a sense of belonging, it is often the "little," basic human things that make major differences. Good teachers have always done things to make their classrooms a welcome place. Many are comfortable greeting students as they come in the room, calling them by name, or simply saying hello with a warm smile. Although simple, these are the kinds of practices that create warmth for all students. We now explore these and similar practices in more depth.

Greet Students

Make it an everyday practice to say hello to each student. If that frequency is unrealistic, then greet each child no less than twice each week. Welcome them as they arrive. Convey the attitude that your classroom is equally their classroom and *you are welcoming them home. Students really appreciate thoughtful gestures from their teachers like a greeting card, a birthday card or a "good job" note. A welcoming smile can be just as effective.*

Call Students by Name

Learn your students' names early and use them often. People are impressed when you know their names, and they feel good when you convey some personal knowledge about them. Further, it is much easier to command respect during disciplinary moments when you know a student's name.

Several teachers have asked for advice about what to do with students who act inappropriately in the hallways between classes. Often they will preface their question by asking for advice in disciplining students they don't know. Our advice is simple: Before getting into the complexities of why a student is misbehaving, first get to know the student's name, then ask him or her to stop.

Know Who Students Are

It is critically important to know your students' interests, perceived strengths, weaknesses, likes, and dislikes. In this way, you can connect with them before frustration leads to withdrawal or aggression. Interest inventories, student surveys, and incomplete sentence forms can elicit a wealth of helpful information in a nonthreatening manner, although some parents may consider this a violation of privacy. Should that be an issue, simply hand out an index card and ask students to write down what makes it hard for them to learn and what helps them learn. By limiting the query to learning, privacy issues are fully respected.

Use Touch and Other Nonverbal Messages

Various studies have found that no more than 10 percent of the meaning of a message is contained in the words spoken. The remaining 90 percent is a combination of nonverbal expression and tone of voice. Some fear that volatile students will misinterpret the meaning of nonverbal messages and react in a violent manner. Many others of us have been warned against touching children because of a growing fear of lawsuits. In 1994, the National Education Association raised the issue of a policy against touching children. While we understand their reasons, the need to nurture many children makes a less-inclusive policy preferable. When educators do not use all of their tools, it is harder to reach and connect with students. Although all but the safest of communications entail some risk, the reality is that most intentions are correctly interpreted. Nonverbal communications will most often enhance relationships in proper ways.

Donna Rogner, a 1st grade teacher in Chicago, resolved this dilemma in a unique way by developing a policy that she called "H or H." She told her children that each day when they entered the room they could have either a hug or a handshake. They could decide and then tell her. She reported that this method was highly effective in getting the day started in the right frame of mind for her group of very difficult children. To our surprise, a 10th grade high school history teacher who was in one of our training seminars tried this method with his students. He privately told us that they loved it! He found it to be a wonderful method to use occasionally (two to three times each month), and he added that if too much time passes, some students will seek him out privately and ask if today will be an "H or H" day.

Since this colleague's experience, we have been challenging middle school and high school teachers to create techniques like this within their own zones of comfort. Most are amazed at their students' receptivity and responsiveness.

You Can Help Us

"Don't let us slip by and say 'Oh well, he's bound for the pen anyway.' Get us involved in our school: in football, or drama, student council, whatever. If there is a need for someone, they, by human nature will answer to that need."

— A male student

Let Them See Who You Are

Students who are turned off to school and are at higher risk of being violent often have very negative associations while in school. For them, teachers are authority figures against whom to rebel. They often ignore or greet high achievement peers in a disdainful way. We need to generate different "movies in their minds" so that they come to see school as important and meaningful. These students especially need us to show a personal interest in them so that they begin to make positive associations with school.

Go to an event when it is likely that one of your students will be present, and greet him or her personally. Identify one or two students who usually make themselves unattractive to you and interact with them in a personal manner for two minutes each day for two consecutive weeks. Acknowledging birthdays and asking about a special piece of clothing or jewelry also helps change a student's point of view.

It can be extremely effective to call high-risk students at home to discuss an issue or to just ask how they are doing. Very often, conflict situations can be resolved in this manner. We send a very strong signal of respect and significance when we think highly enough about a student to take our own personal time to call. The message is powerful and often transforms their perceptions when students hear such statements as: "Joe, I was upset in class today and I thought this might be a good time for us to put our heads together and come up with a solution that will work for both of us." Or, "Mike, threatening to cut up my tires tells me that you are extremely mad. Although I've thought about calling the police, what I really want is for you to help me understand what I did that made you so upset. I thought this would be a good time to talk it over."

There is both safety and intimacy over the phone. The phone provides a safe barrier for students who need distance or who present in a physically threatening manner. The teacher is able to get within earshot of a student who otherwise may react negatively to close proximity. Finally, the phone provides privacy. There are no other students to attract through inappropriate behavior or who are around to comment on the interaction.

Teach to Diverse Learning Styles and Multiple Intelligences

With his theory of multiple intelligences, Howard Gardner (1983) postulates the existence of seven distinct intelligences. He claims that only two of these are highlighted in school. Those with high linguistic (word analysis and usage) or math intelligence (logical reasoning) tend to do very well because schools usually emphasize these content areas. In contrast, students with high "body" (kinesthetic) and musical intelligence tend to get into trouble more often because of their need for movement. For example, we tend to assume that the pencil tapper or rapper is being disruptive rather than viewing her as needing, feeling, or expressing an inner rhythm. By expanding our definition of what constitutes intelligence, more students will be included in the learning process and school can become a less frustrating place.

We often ask teachers who attend our seminars to think back to a class that they found difficult as a student. They knew that this class wasn't a strength, but they had to be there anyway. We then ask these same educators to imagine that their entire school experience existed in that class and that all future classes would be similar. These images are usually sufficient to help colleagues feel how it is to be in a place where expectations don't match strengths.

We would do well to incorporate into our daily curriculums learning experiences based upon what students have told us they find motivating. Among the practical approaches most students find motivating are interviewing people, making collections of things related to concepts presented in the classroom, going on field trips that integrate actual and academic experiences, working on projects with peers, acting things out, and conducting independent experiments (Goodlad 1984, 1994). The work of Armstrong (1993, 1994) and Lazear (1991) provides educators with many practical ways of integrating instruction so that children with diverse strengths can benefit. When we are truly serious about including and noticing all students, we might even adopt unconventional solutions. For example, Kuykendall (1992), offers the possibility of schools establishing comedy clubs so that class clowns have a sanctioned outlet for attention and fun.

Focus on Academic Competence

Since academic achievement is the primary yardstick that many students use to measure their self-worth in school, educators must devise ways of helping each student become an academic winner. It is no surprise that the vast majority of troubled students who cause trouble in school are among the academically unsuccessful. They often decide that there is much more honor in acting "bad" than in looking "stupid." Others just toss in the towel quietly while rage builds inside. It is essential that we use practices that prevent students from becoming discouraged learners, or use effective interventions when they are discouraged, so that a real sense of self-worth fueled by genuine accomplishment can build confidence. The following are proven ways:

Ensure Success. A 5th grade teacher turned around the behavior of several students in her class by simply changing one important approach. Any time she asks a question, the student to whom the question is asked owns the question. She continues interacting with that student until either that or a related question has been successfully answered. In this way, students learn to anticipate being successful. Disruptive behavior in this class dramatically decreased, and class participation dramatically improved.

When I recently visited a high school math class, one student gave a wrong answer. I watched with great curiosity as the teacher worked with the student for several minutes until she understood how to do the problem correctly. Later, I asked the teacher why he spent so much time with that one student. He told me that it was his job to ensure that all students understand the material. He stated, "While I know that I can't always devote the time during class, it is my job to do everything possible, short of doing the work or taking the tests for them, so that students, even reluctant ones, get the knowledge they need!"

Highlight Effort. I recently observed a homogeneously grouped class of low achievers who had gained a negative reputation among teachers in the school. As I watched these children go from class to class, I was struck by their obvious need to show that they didn't care. Many came unprepared, several collected zeroes, and more than a few were quick to challenge authority. Yet they behaved very differently with Mrs. Lorenz, their social studies teacher. I noticed that consistently, in a genuine way, she made each of her students feel safe for the efforts they made. As she returned an assignment to a student who had received 60 percent, she said, "You did a great job on questions, 1, 6, 7, 8, 9, and 10. But I noticed that you didn't do the others. Those have to do with exports. I must not have done a very good job teaching that. I'll be reviewing exports in the first few minutes of today's class, and then you can do these others if you'd like to improve your grade. Either way, congratulations on the answers you completed. They were done very well!" In her class, the difficult students were highly motivated, concerned about their performance, and eager to improve.

Encourage Mistakes. In her book *My Posse Don't Do Homework*, LouAnne Johnson (1992) describes a situation where she is teaching "The Taming of the Shrew" to a challenging, academically underachieving class. She asks a question and no one answers. Finally, after a few minutes of silence, a boy "without a shred of confidence" gives an answer. He is a boy who rarely answers and almost never volunteers. Johnson, in disbelief, wants to pat him on the back. But as she approaches, he sinks into his seat, embarrassed. She reaches into her pocket, pulls out a dollar bill, and gives it to the boy. He looks at her and says, "Was that right?" She answers, "No, but that's not important." Another student challenges, "How come he gets a dollar for a wrong answer?" She answers, "Because sometimes it takes a lot of wrong answers before you get the right one. But if you're afraid to think, you'll never figure anything out" (p. 186).

While payment for risking wrong answers has its own problems (including going broke!), the larger point is to find ways of encouraging students to take appropriate risks that expand their knowledge and make them hunger for more.

It takes a love of learning to genuinely rejoice in the mistakes of our students. We know a teacher who regularly thanks students for making errors. She'll enthusiastically tell the class, "Tanika made an excellent mistake. She did the whole long division problem correctly except she added instead of subtracted. That serves as a good reminder that we can know how to do something well, but paying attention to those little things like plus and minus signs can make a difference. Thanks for making that mistake Tanika. We can all learn from it."

One of the principles of Project Essential (Ewing Marion Kauffman Foundation 1995), a Kansas City-based self-esteem program that is yielding impressive results, is that we all make errors and can learn from them. As early as kindergarten, children are taught to think and say, "Oops, I goofed!" when they make cognitive or social mistakes. It is impressive to watch students more willingly risk and eagerly learn in such classrooms.

Focus on the Positive, Especially When It's Hard to Find. Some students are hard to appreciate. They irritate and know exactly what buttons to press and how to press them for maximum irritation. It is easy to understand the desire to withdraw or fight with such students. Yet, we must remember that their angry, negative ways often reflect their own self-hatred and their misguided life events, not ours. While interacting with these students can be unappealing, it is our professional responsibility to never give up searching for ways that may turn them around. Wise teachers invest preventive time by calling or writing regularly to students and their parents at home to share appreciations, ask for suggestions, and provide feedback.

Johnson (1992) describes another student, Callie, as an attention-seeking, disruptive girl who yawned loudly while looking straight into her teacher's eyes. Sweet smiles and insincere apologies would follow. Johnson decided to write Callie's parents a note telling them how much she enjoyed having her in class and that she was a bright student with a delightful sense of humor and a B average. She handed the note to the girl, unsealed, and asked that it be given to her parents. Callie never yawned in class again.

Mr. Parselli had done all of the usual consequences in efforts to "motivate" Jose to come to class on time. He talked with him, called home, gave late slips and detention, and kicked him out of class. It was all to no avail. Frustrated by Jose's continued tardiness, Mr. Parselli used an unexpected method. Such methods are designed to promote a sense of confusion or surprise because an unusual response has been given to a predictable situation.

To use paradoxical methods, it is necessary for the teacher to depersonalize the student's inappropriate behavior. The teacher also must adopt the attitude that the student is more important than his or her behavior. It is a variation on Haim Ginott's (1976) focus on valuing the person while disapproving of the behavior. In this case, Mr. Parselli approached Jose after class and said, "Jose, I would like you to be in class on time, but for reasons I don't understand, that is not happening. I want you to know that even though I am not happy that you come late, you are an important member of our class. I can see that you listen, you sometimes give an answer, and you are often friendly. If there is anything that I can do to help you get here earlier, please let me know. If not, I'd rather see you late than not at all."

Growing numbers of students who lack adequate nurturing and attention will resist change when they don't trust. Because people are often frightened by change, they are more apt to take a risk when they are not forced to let go of the familiar. In the presence of an encouraging teacher who invites but does not demand change, many youth will try on an alternative behavior because they know that they will be accepted either way. In Jose's case, change was not possible because as the oldest of several children in a single-parent family, he was responsible for seeing the younger children off to school. While Jose continued to come late, Mr. Parselli reported a marked improvement in his attitude after their talk.

Have Fun

Classrooms with warmth are notable for their emphasis on fun and enjoyment. A growing body of research indicates that fun leads to or is part of high classroom achievement. Colwell and Wigle (1984) note that humor may be a motivational device for reluctant learners. Whitmer (1986) explains how to use humorous literature to teach critical reading. Vance (1987) found that if the interest or arousal level of a group was low, the use of humor to introduce the lesson raised these levels so teaching and learning took place. With so much anger and depression in the lives of children, school can become a refuge where escape into fun is an important part of the planned experience.

Allow yourself to laugh, and permit your students to enjoy being with you and each other. We believe that every educator ought to do at least one planned enjoyable activity with every class each day.

Listen, Listen, and Then Listen Some More

We are convinced that most problems that interfere with learning would never occur if each student had at least one important adult in his or her life who regularly listened with caring and concern and *without* judgment. If every child had 10 minutes a day with this caring adult who listened about victories, defeats, joys, and hurts, the power of connection would override most other factors.

We cannot provide this for all students to the extent that it is needed. But we can offer our willingness to connect by noticing the realities that our students face. All that may be needed is a tone of concern expressed to a student who walks in with a grumpy face. For example, if you see a student with a grumpy face, asking how things are going with a caring, concerned voice lets him know that he is not alone.

Some children and teenagers do better when they can write down their joys and frustrations and share them with someone who cares. In the classroom, there are many small ways to accomplish this. Put out a suggestion box and invite students to offer ways to make the class a more satisfying place. Assure them that you will either implement their suggestions or tell them why you won't or can't. All suggestions that are signed can be treated in this way. To avoid silly or offensive suggestions, give students language parameters that they must respect. All unsigned suggestions may or may not warrant feedback. Set aside time to answer the perennial question "Why do we need to know that?" Invite older students to keep a journal; younger students can color about their feelings.

A middle-school teacher in one of our sessions recently shared her strategy of offering all students "two days off" each semester. If she detects that a student is agitated, overwhelmed, or burned out, she suggests a day off. A student may request a day off when he or she believes it's needed. The student remains in class and is expected to be nondisruptive but is not required to actively participate.

Tommy Smith, a middle school teacher in Orlando, Florida, has a "baggage box" in his classroom. He explains to students that everyone carries "baggage" (problems) and that from time to time this baggage may be so heavy that it gets in the way of learning and concentrating. When students bring their "baggage" to class, he encourages them to anonymously write about what is bugging them, place it in a sealed envelope, and put it in the box. At the end of class, students may reclaim their baggage or leave it. All old baggage is discarded at the end of the day. Many students take advantage of leaving their baggage behind. Those who want to reclaim their baggage put a symbol on the outside of the sealed envelope to denote ownership. To assure privacy, if they want it back, they must show the symbol they used on a separate paper to Mr. Smith, who then retrieves the envelope. It is rare for students to reclaim their note.

Teach Empathy

The best way of building a sense of community among all students is to model and encourage displays of empathy in the classroom. One of the most powerful things an educator can do is simple, but requires courage: apologize. When we blow it and know it, an apology expresses genuine remorse that is essential to the development of conscience and empathy.

A high school teacher recently shared his graphic "MY I" strategy that he uses with his "general" class. Each week, Mr. Aziz draws a full body self-portrait and pins it to his shirt. The words "MY I" are written on the portrait to convey ownership as he lets his students know that words and deeds can either be supportive or disrespectful. When his students say or do things to him that he considers disrespectful, he takes a scissors and cuts off a body part to note injury. His original goal was to get through a day with at least one body part remaining. Four weeks into this practice, improvement was so dramatic that on average only two body parts each week were trimmed.

The concrete symbol of a person being cut served as a powerful point of awareness and source of learning. It became common for students to ask him what they had done when he cut off a body part. He learned that most of the time his students did not intend disrespect. Their statements reflected the "in your face" society so prevalent in the United States. He later expanded this practice so that students participated in like fashion.

Mrs. Hanson, a high school special education teacher, creates a "hot seat" in her classroom. Any student with a gripe towards another can request "hot seat" time. While in the hot seat, the offended student gets to tell his or her view of an incident and express his or her feelings. The accused student is given an opportunity to respond. This continues back and forth until both sides have expressed themselves. The class remains present so that everyone observes. After the aggrieved students have had their say, the class participates in brainstorming solutions that will improve the situation. Mrs. Hanson reports that many of her juniors and seniors encourage the younger students to take advantage of this problem-solving opportunity.

An elementary teacher we met models patience with her young children by writing PATIENCE on the chalkboard each day. She teaches about the virtue of showing patience as well as the frustration we feel and the time we lose when we act in ways that upset people's patience. Then she explains that when things happen in class that challenge her patience, she will erase one letter at a time. Letters left at the end of the day are traded for extra play activities as both a token of appreciation and consequence of thoughtfulness.

On a regular basis, empathy is taught by placing students who seem not to care about others in positions to help either people or pets. Usually, they need to be supervised because students lacking empathy have often been emotionally wounded and abused. They have shut down to people as a means of protection. They also may harbor resentment for the hurts they have experienced and are therefore at greater risk of hurting or abusing others.

Many hurting students are reawakened to empathy through supervised experiences in which caring is requisite. For example, we worked with juvenile delinquent youth who became actual clowns and then entertained children at nursery schools and seniors at a nursing home. Many of these boys became more sensitive through this experience, as they realized the positive effects their behavior could have on others. We believe that street-toughened kids can make excellent mentors for severely disabled children and the elderly. Preliminary anecdotal reports indicate a very good fit between these groups.

We have observed difficult, oppositional youth who are mentors willingly performing such basic functions as feeding and changing diapers. At school, challenging students can be offered supervised "big brother" opportunities in which they help a younger child in need.

Though all of the activities above can help, there is no exact formula that nurtures warmth in a classroom. Much depends upon attitude and intentions. Warm classrooms have teachers who deliver interesting lessons that connect with students. These teachers have a sense of humor and instruct with a personal touch. Their classroom conveys a sense of ownership for everybody.

The words of Jorge Alemo, a teacher in San Antonio, Texas, provide a good picture of how warmth affects learning and behavior.

> As a kid growing up in West San Antonio attending a 99 percent Hispanic school, I respected the teacher that provided a positive attitude coupled with fair discipline. I respected the teacher that disciplined me fairly and respected me. I was very shy back then but I was full of pride. I would think positive things but I would keep them to myself. To teachers that were disrespectful I would give the silent treatment. I did not like being yelled at or made to feel inadequate. ... [Now, as a teacher,] I respect and acknowledge the existence of students each day. I model the respect that every human should expect. I seek to learn from them. In conducting my class, I follow the guidelines of retail management. I believe that every teacher should be a salesperson. The classroom is a store. In order to make a sale/ teach, the students must understand the information, like what they hear and see, and be able to picture themselves with a better life because of what they have learned.

Questions and Suggestions for Building Warmth in the Classroom

Since there are a multitude of ways to build warmth in your school, the key is to identify practices that are compatible with who you are. By connecting the practice with your style, genuineness is the result. We offer some questions and suggestions to help you get clear about what you want to do.

1. When you visit someone in their home, what are some things they do that help you feel welcome?

2. What are some practices that others do that help you feel welcome in their home that are applicable in the classroom?

3. What teachers did you have when you were in school that made you feel special or important? What did they do that gave you that feeling?

4. Identify at least three practices that you can do to promote a sense of connection with your students in the classroom.

5. Think of one or two students you currently have that you find unattractive. Are you willing to devote two minutes each day for two weeks with at least one of these students in an effort to develop a more meaningful relationship?

6. Visit at least three other teachers in your school while they are teaching. Identify practices that you see them doing that you consider to be good ways of building warmth.

7. Think of one or two students you currently have that create problems in the classroom who appear to be of relatively high influence in the eyes of their peers. These students are often effective at influencing "wannabes" to join their behaviors. Call at least one of them at home to discuss your concerns in an effort to find solutions.

Clearly Defined Limits

Students need secure, confident, respectful adults who are appropriately confrontational when they go over the line. In earlier books, we wrote about the importance of having clear and specific rules that are connected to a set of principles or values that define the classroom atmosphere (Curwin and Mendler 1988, Mendler 1992, Curwin 1992). Readers who want specific step-by-step guidelines in establishing school or classroom rules are referred to these earlier works. We focus in this section on ways for educators to interact with students so that the implementation of rules is most effective. Our observations lead us to believe that how we do things is much more important than what we do. A good rule that is connected to its principle but poorly implemented is much less effective than a poor rule that is enforced effectively. The best practice is to have good rules that are effectively enforced.

Schools need to be "safety zones" with policies that provide for the safety of students and are made public and repeated as often as necessary. Within the classroom, each teacher should emphatically support principles of nonviolence, have rules that support these principles, and then teach students appropriate alternatives for expressing anger and frustration.

The most effective and respected teachers express their beliefs, demands, and expectations within the context of clear values and goals. They have found a way to be firm and hold students accountable while treating them with dignity and maintaining their own dignity.

Many teachers are faced with impulsive students whose hostility can quickly escalate. We must learn and remind ourselves how to enforce rules without threats while being both assertive and respectful.

Don't Threaten

Students who are out of control do not respond favorably to threats. An alternative is to use active listening. If a student says that he is going to slash your tires, it is best to say something like, "That would be very upsetting. I need my tires, and I can see how angry you are! Let's see if we can find a different way to settle this." Remember that being emotional in a tense situation usually conveys a lack of self-control.

Prudence is advisable as well. If need be, alert school security or the police. Do it, don't threaten! Threats are easily disguised as warnings or choices. No teacher ever says, "You better stop, I'm threatening you!" Instead they say, "I'm warning you!" Children know that it is not the words but the intentions that define a threat. Be sure your choices are not simply veiled threats that are made of two alternatives: Do what I want or I'll punish you. These types of veiled choices often elicit violent countermeasures, particularly with students who become easily agitated.

Use P.E.P. (Privacy/Eye-Contact/Proximity)

We have repeatedly found that a confrontation with an audience exacerbates explosive situations. When a student who is prone to violence breaks a rule, it is best to quietly and privately talk with that student (privacy). Be near the student (proximity) and make nonthreatening eye contact (eye contact). The latter may be forsaken if students get defensive and refuse eye contact. Cultural and emotional issues are often at the root of such refusals, and it is simply wiser to communicate in a respectful manner with privacy and proximity than to force eye contact. P.E.P. works best when it is periodically used to convey messages of appreciation as well as correction.

Say No Respectfully

How we say things is often more important than what we say. Some years ago, we worked with a personnel director in a school district who had the unenviable task of telling teachers that they were being laid off during an especially tight fiscal time. It was remarkable that this man's caring manner and supportive words had these very teachers extolling his virtues after he broke the news.

In any classroom, part of the job of the teacher is to say no. When we do, it is important that we maintain the dignity of the student to protect our relationship with the child and to sustain the student's motivation. Simply saying no and offering your best reason in a concise manner is effective and appreciated: "If I said yes or allowed that to go on, I wouldn't be doing my job. My job is to make sure that we respect each other and cooperate together."

Assert Yourself

Mary Cantrell (1992) cites the research of C. Ronald Huff, who suggests that fear invites intimidation. After a two-year study of Ohio youth gangs, Huff said, "Contrary to much 'common wisdom,' teachers who demonstrate that they care about a youth and then are firm and fair in their expectations are rarely, if ever, the victims of assaults by gang members. Rather, it is those teachers who 'back down' and are easily intimidated who are more likely to be the victims of assault. During two years of interviews, not one gang member ever said that a teacher who insisted on academic performance (within the context of a caring relationship) was assaulted. Such teachers are respected far more than those perceived as weak. 'Weakness' generally represents a quality to be exploited by gang members in an almost Darwinian fashion, much as they select targets on the street."

To be verbally assertive, use I-Messages that tell another person what is bothersome and what you want instead. For example, "Joe, I appreciate that you pound your fist on the desk rather than on someone's head. That shows self-control. I'd also like to discuss nonpounding ways of saying when you are annoyed."

Convey nonverbal assertiveness through body language that includes an upright posture, free-swinging arms while moving, and head up with firm yet nonthreatening eye contact. When working with violence-prone youth, it is beneficial to take a class in self-defense if for no other reason than knowing that you can defend yourself against physical attack. That builds confidence that makes it less likely that you will ever need to use such skills.

You Can Help Us

"I don't think much can be done to absolutely eliminate violence, but if there is no time to commit an act of violence, then an act of violence can't be committed."

— A male student

Johnson (1992) talks about her first day on the job in a class that had eaten up three earlier teachers. She relates a story about an altercation with a group of burly high schoolers, one of whom had just thrown a large dictionary that barely missed her head.

> I closed my eyes for a few seconds and mentally transported myself back to Marine boot camp, where I had met my first instructor. Barely five feet tall, she had the presence of a giant. Her primary weapon was her eyes. When she looked at you, you knew you were being looked at, inside and out. I prepared myself to make my students feel 100 percent visible. . . . I opened my eyes and marched down the center aisle toward the young man who had thrown the dictionary. I didn't slow my pace as I neared him. When I approached, his friends edged to each side, and he tried to step backward. . . . I stopped a few inches in front of him. "Excuse me," I said, biting the tip off each word. "I would appreciate it if you would sit down. . . . " He held my gaze for about two minutes but couldn't handle my close presence. . . . Finally he cleared his throat and asked where I wanted him to sit. . . . I stepped aside and pointed toward the front seats. Then I flashed him a bright smile and added, "Thank you very much, young man." (p. 25)

Questions and Suggestions for Clearly Defined Limits

Take a few moments to begin reflecting on specific rules that you think are necessary for good learning and teaching to occur. Identify the value or principle that guides the rule. Discipline is best when students know what to do (rules) and why it is necessary (values/principles). The questions that follow can help you get clear about creating effective rules that are based on principles that support learning.

1. What rules do you expect students to follow? Be specific.

2. How do these rules support learning? Imagine your students are in front of you. Tell them how you think their learning will improve by following the rules.

3. What are the values or principles that support your rules? We have found that rules only make sense when students understand and value the principles upon which they are based. At-risk students become especially angered when they view rules as arbitrary and controlling. List your values (such as, All students should solve their problems nonviolently, We value respectful behavior when we disagree with each other) and then the specific rules you think are necessary. These should each be congruent with the value.

Democratic Atmosphere

Explosive and potentially dangerous students often feel powerless. But there are ways of signaling and demonstrating to them that they have influence over what happens to them, and that their input at school is valued and important. In our *Discipline with Dignity* program (Curwin and Mendler 1988), we have long advocated that schools involve students positively as decision makers and problem solvers. They can be invited to assist in developing values, principles, rules, and even consequences in the classroom. When problems occur, student input is often helpful. That gives them an important sense of involvement and ownership which often translates into commitment and responsibility. It is not unusual for some of the most difficult youngsters to become class "behavior monitors" when empowered in this way. They begin to monitor each other and eventually themselves.

When students realize that their thoughts and opinions are valued and may be important enough to influence policy, students participate in a democratic process. Becoming skilled at making decisions while realizing that some will be supported while others are not is an essential life skill for success in a democratic culture.

Teachers need to realize that a growing number of students have little actual control in their lives. Students need us to help them feel in control. Listening to them and giving them a say in the routines, activities, and rules that affect them at school can make a positive difference. Following are some ways to involve students.

Invite Students to Develop Principles for the Class

Because the most effective rules are developed from principles and values, the first step for empowering students and involving them in the structural processes of the class is to have them express their values and ideals. All rules will be developed from the list of these principles. The teacher will often get the discussion started by using schoolwide principles or rules as a guide (e.g., "The school policy states that no weapons are permitted on campus and may be grounds for expulsion. Why do you think we need a rule like this at school?"). The teacher can also use his own needs to frame the conversation (e.g., "I have a hard time teaching when folks call out answers and interrupt each other. Why might it be important to you for others to not interrupt while you are speaking?").

Have Students Develop Rules for the Teacher

This allows students to express their expectations for their teacher. The teacher leads the process by asking students to create rules that he or she will follow to help them learn. Rules must be clear and specific, behavioral, and related to educationally sound values. Teachers have two choices for those infrequent times when students propose unacceptable rules. The first is to veto the rule. There is no override allowed for a teacher veto, although it is critical that an explanation accompany the veto. Otherwise, students may see the process as bogus. It is rarely necessary to veto when the appropriate criteria have been used (i.e., the rule must **help** you learn or **not interfere** with the learning process). Some criteria for vetoing are:

- The rule violates a schoolwide rule or a law.
- The rule does not match one of the teacher's important values (thus reinforcing the link between values and rules, and model ing the having of values).
- The rule interferes with the learning process.

The second choice when the teacher is uncomfortable with the rule is to give it a trial for a limited time. For example, if students propose "no homework," the teacher may put the rule on trial for as long as one week while developing a simple system to evaluate the effectiveness of the rule. She might give a daily quiz on the content of the homework and allow only those students who demonstrate success on the quiz to continue with the rule. Obviously, this option is limited to proposed rules that the teacher views as undesirable but *not dangerous*.

Have Students Develop Rules for Each Other

Students are more likely to follow rules that are important to them and that they create. In addition, developing rules is an excellent beginning for learning responsibility, understanding the concept of limits, and feeling in control. Ideas can be discussed during class or in small groups, or by submitting suggestions individually. For example, as a homework assignment, the teacher might ask students to think of rules that are important. A cumulative list can then be developed to guide further discussion. The same criteria apply for student rules for the class as for student rules for the teacher. They should be clear and specific, behavioral, and related to educationally sound values. Once again, it is okay to stretch your boundaries, but do not accept rules you cannot live with.

Allow Students to Vote on Negotiable Rules

It might be better for young students or those with very little practice in generating ideas from scratch to vote on a set of rules developed by the teacher. These rules should consist of guidelines that aren't absolutely necessary in order to run the classroom effectively. The distinction is between rules that are essential and therefore non-negotiable (e.g., hitting) and those that are important but unessential (e.g., seating preferences, responsibilities for classroom routines). The teacher shares responsibility but does not surrender authority in this process. Her long-range view of the academic goals as well as insistence, when necessary, upon interpersonal decency guides the discussion. The teacher must be open to other points of view, encourage sharing, and stay focused on the educational goals that need to be achieved.

After the Teacher Defines Principles and Values, Have Students Develop the Rules

This variation allows students to develop specific rules based upon the teacher's principles. The teacher emphasizes the purposes of the rules by focusing on the values that are most essential, while the students do most of the work in creating or modifying the rules. The teacher and students also could collaboratively share the responsibility for developing both principles and rules.

We have found that what matters most is meaningful student involvement. The actual processes used are at the discretion of the teacher and should reflect his or her beliefs and comfort.

Do Specific Problem Solving with Students

Here are some questions for developing a democratic atmosphere:

1. Which suggestions are you most comfortable with regarding student development of rules and principles?

2. Think of the various procedures and routines that exist in the classroom. Which of these could be offered to students for their input?

3. To whom do you believe the responsibility for behavior in the classroom belongs?

4. What strategies can you think of that would help you promote responsible behavior through student involvement and ownership among those you identified?

5. Think of a student who is disruptive with classmates and with whom your efforts have had minimal success. You have already talked with colleagues and parents (if available) to seek solutions. Consider presenting your concerns to a group of mature students from the classroom and invite them to brainstorm possible solutions. What is the best way to present your concerns?

When problems persist with one or more students, there is little doubt that all others in the class are negatively affected. While we view the educator as the classroom leader, he or she is not the only one responsible for defining and maintaining standards. Students can be extremely effective in using their collective powers of persuasion upon those who interfere with the learning process.

When safety is the issue, students need either assurance or reassurance that their teacher will be the primary person in the classroom who will handle the situation. But students also can be involved as partners in solving problems when they occur in the classroom. In this way, they learn responsibility by practicing it. Establishing basic problem-solving procedures and then using them can be very effective. We suggest the following:

1. Ask students what is "good" about the problem. This will require them to define the problem clearly. For example, "What is good about calling people names? What is good about being called a name?" We begin with asking about what is good about a problem because that helps students see the benefits derived from the situation. Problems rarely get solved until people realize and understand what sustains the problem behavior.

2. Ask students what is "bad" about the problem. This will give them a chance to express how their learning and perhaps safety is threatened by the problem or the problem student. For example, "What is bad about calling people names? What is bad about being called a name?"

3. List all possible solutions to the problem. Use basic brainstorming procedures, then list all possible solutions. These may cover: suggestions for the teacher to solve the problem, suggestions for students to help solve the problem, suggestions for the problem student to solve the problem, or suggestions for others in school or outside to help solve the problem.

4. Decide on the best possible solution.

Recognizing and Resolving Conflict

I recently met a preschool teacher who told me about a 4-year-old child who constantly used guns in his play. He drew guns, built guns with Legos, and talked about guns. Her efforts to prohibit such play were met with even more intense aggressive play. She was understandably concerned that other children would become aggressive, and she was trying to promote an atmosphere of cooperation and nonviolence.

When I asked her if she knew much about this child's background with guns, she dejectedly told me that he had seen his cousin killed, and that his uncle was the recent victim of a drive-by shooting that took place in his home. The child was in the next room when this happened.

It was clear from our discussion that this young child was stressed, frightened, and preoccupied with these events and was reliving some or all of this through his play. In effect, he had no other place to turn for safety and meaning than to his play. His teacher needed help in seeing that to really give this child a sense of control, she needed to find ways to engage his need for guns within his play. Engaging a student means being a good listener who is willing to explore, work with, and attempt to understand the meaning of troubling behavior. I encouraged her to do a lot of "active listening" by following the themes that the child set. He needed to be engaged by someone who cared and was able to decode his messages. He needed to know that she would do everything she could to make sure he felt safe in the classroom. Eventually, the child's preoccupation with guns diminished, at least temporarily, though the absence of a strong emotional support network made his eventual outcome far from certain.

With so many children experiencing crises on an almost daily basis, we must reframe our concept of the classroom to include affirmation and validation of their real life experiences. Often, this may be painful and distasteful to us, because the decision to care means engaging rather than withdrawing from emotionally unpleasant experiences. Since wounded students who externalize their pain often project it onto those who are closest, we need to be prepared for their expressions of anger, torment, frustration, and humiliation.

The most helpful and effective response is for us to stand up without fighting back. We must let students know that we find their behavior objectionable, but that we are able to look beyond it while at the same time preserving our dignity and the integrity of a classroom full of shocked, wondering students. The major challenge with students who provoke us is to find ways to stay personally involved without personalizing their misery. Students who attack are virtually always under attack themselves. If they are attacked back, the never-ending cycle perpetuates itself. Since these students see the world as a hostile place, they often set others up to reject them so that their world view is confirmed. When we continue to care and refuse to give up, it is common for them to push harder and harder until finally they surrender to the possibility of bonding. It is not an easy process, but it is one that can be wonderfully rewarding at the end of the road. Most important, as professional educators, we must behave as if we can make a difference with all students. It is not for us to predetermine who will make it and who will not, who is worth the effort and who is not, who will wind up successful and who will be the next criminal. Our job is to teach *all* of the children. In reality, we won't reach them all, and there are some from whom we need breaks from the stress we feel when working with them. But in the end, we must stay dedicated to believing that change is possible and that our efforts may make the difference.

It is important to recognize that troubled students make us mad and stressed. They get to us because they are experienced in getting people to dislike them. It is important that we unwind by permitting ourselves to honestly and privately express these frustrations. We benefit by taking good emotional care of ourselves. We also benefit from periodic vacations from these students. It can be helpful to develop a support network with colleagues (including use of each other's classroom) that gives us space from belligerent students for brief periods. We are at our best when we work hard and are dedicated to not giving up.

Be prepared for power struggles. Difficult students test our resolve by trying to embarrass and engage us in battle in the classroom. It requires great courage and much skill to stand up and not fight back. Most problem moments can be defused through a combination of listening to the student's thoughts and feelings, acknowledging the student's concern, agreeing that there may be some truth in the student's accusation, and deferring to a private time for continued discussion.

Continuing to care and not give up means that we have to be well prepared and skilled in knowing what to do when students challenge authority. The goal is to resolve the immediate conflict so that attention can be returned to instruction as quickly as possible. The educator's response should be guided by preservation of the student's dignity, a display of assertiveness that shows the ability to stand up to conflict and not fight back, efforts to keep the student in class, and the use of strategies that students can use when they are confronted with similar conflict. Rarely are conflicts solved for the long-term in the presence of an audience, but effective responses are required to defuse problem situations so that instruction can continue when a student challenges in class. We offer a series of specific suggestions that are designed to defuse students when they attempt to provoke conflict.

Specific Suggestions for Defusing and Resolving Conflict

1. When you need to offer corrective feedback to students, us P.E.P. if at all possible (privacy, eye contact, proximity). Most students won't fight when their prestige is preserved. Keeping the message between the two of you is the one best way to make your point effectively while maintaining everyone's dignity.

2. Ask or tell the student politely but clearly what you want. Use the words "please" and "thank you" without begging (e.g., "Bill, please use different words when you speak in class. I will really appreciate your cooperation. Thanks.").

3. Actively listen to what the student is saying without agreeing or disagreeing (e.g., "I know you're mad if you're using words like those. Let's get together later and figure things out.").

4. Actively listen to the student's feelings without agreeing or disagreeing (e.g., "You are really big-time upset. Hang in there a little while longer. Thanks.").

5. Tell the student that a power struggle is brewing and defer further discussion until a private time (e.g., "Juan, you're angry and so am I. Rather than get into an argument that won't solve our problem, let's calm down and talk later. I'm sure we can help each other out if we try harder in a little while.").

6. Ask the student to leave the classroom or, if that's not possible, take a time out somewhere in the classroom (e.g., Leah, right now I'm torn between solving our problem and teaching this book to the rest of the class, and it looks like you aren't ready to solve the problem with me. Please go to Mrs. Hanshee's classroom. There is a seat there for you. Come back when you're ready to learn. I hope that doesn't take very long.").

7. In extreme cases (e.g., the student refuses to leave, there's no help available in the office), invite the student to either stop the behavior or assume the responsibility for teaching for a short time. Role reversals can be effective in these extreme cases.

Let's look to actually see how to apply these suggestions. Mrs. Lewis is a third of the way through her lesson when she sees Joe beginning to tap a pencil on his desk. As she continues teaching, she walks toward Joe and quietly takes a moment to ask him to stop tapping (P.E.P.), "Joe, that's a neat rhythm, but it's distracting the other students. I need you to stop."

You Can Help Us

"I also think that parents need to be more involved with their children. They need to be a part of their lives more. Metal detectors and such help protect students, but it doesn't solve the problem."

— A female student

Joe says: "I'm not the only one. Why are you always picking on me?"

"Joe, you think I'm being unfair right now. Is that right?" (active listening)

"Yeah, every time I do something, you're always pickin' on me. How come you ain't never botherin' Felipe?"

Mrs. Lewis answers, "Joe, you must feel hurt and mad to think that I'm always after you. Let's talk about this later when we can figure out a good solution." (active listening with feeling, and deferring to a private time)

But Joe replies, "I can't stay later, and I'm just sick of this. How come you're picking on me?"

"Joe, I know you're mad, but if we keep this up, I know we'll wind up in a fight. Let's get together later when we can work this out." (more active listening and deferring to a private time)

"I don't have to if I don't want to!"

"You are right, Joe," Mrs. Lewis answers. "I can't make you. The real question is whether you can make yourself stop so that we can work this out without fighting." (agreeing and deferring)

"This class s——s!!"

"Joe, please stop or leave the class if you must. I hope you decide to stay, but if you don't, I'll understand. My offer still stands. Let's meet later when we can work this out." (leaving the class; deferring to a private time)

"Stuff it!!! I'm not leaving and you can't make me!!"

"Joe, I can't teach right now while we're arguing, so why don't you take over for a few minutes, and when you're done, I'll continue. (Gives up control of class for a short time. At this point the teacher needs to either get help, ask a student to get help, or do role reversal in which the teacher sits in Joe's seat while Joe teaches.)

It is important to realize that when educators stay focused on the goal of defusing, rarely is it necessary to move beyond the active listening phases.

To summarize, the best way of dealing with prospective power struggles is to avoid them. P.E.P. is the best way. When that is ineffective, some combination of listening, acknowledging, agreeing, or deferring will be effective most of the time.

The key is to remain in control when someone is blaming or becoming angry. The concept of staying personal without personalizing the behavior is especially needed in the heat of conflict. Finally, it is necessary to stand up to the assault without fighting back. In addition to the skills already described, we offer the following examples of words or sentences that often are effective when combined with the correct attitude. It is important to realize that each of these sentences is only an example that may or may not work for you. You need to find your words and, more importantly, define your own delivery, including body language, tone of voice, and speed to convey a calm, confident, professional attitude that is welcoming and assertive without being intimidating.

Practice in the Use of Defusing Skills

Imagine that a student is in class and challenges your authority by saying or doing something offensive and inappropriate. Read each of the examples below. Say each out loud at least a few times while imagining that you are actually talking to the student. Realize that some of these sentences will never be appropriate for you because of who you are. Others may fit right away. For most, some degree of practice will be necessary before you will be able to decide whether or not the statement can be made genuinely—and it is important to be genuine for these sentences to be effective. Children know when you are manipulating rather than communicating. Sincerity is more important than content.

At the same time, we need to realize that difficult students make us mad, which challenges our skill at remaining calm, anger-free, and genuine. That is why it is important to practice a skill before you are actually ready for implementation.

Defusing Statements that Avoid Power Struggles

- I'm disappointed that you are choosing to use such angry words even though I'm sure there is much to be upset about.
- I know there is a solution to this, but I don't know what it is right now. Let's meet later when we can really figure this out.
- Your words (actions) tell me you are bored. It takes a lot of discipline to hang in there when you are unsure about why we are doing certain things. Thanks for hanging in there.
- I know you are angry, but there is no problem too big that can't be solved. Let's use words to solve the problem.
- You're just not yourself today, and that must feel lousy.
- We both know there are other ways of telling how we feel while still being respectful. I look forward to hearing from you after class.
- Throwing books (chairs, clothes) doesn't make problems disappear. It only creates new ones. Let's use our words to say why we feel so mad!
- I really want to understand what I did to bother you. But swearing at me doesn't help. Let's talk later when we can be alone.
- Wow, you must be feeling awfully mad to use those words in front of everyone. Let's talk later when we can work this out.
- You must be mad to embarrass me like this in front of everyone. It makes me want to fight back, but then we'd never solve the problem. Later is the time to handle this.
- I'm glad you trust me enough to tell me how you feel and I'm concerned. Any suggestions for improvement are appreciated.
- There may be some truth to what you are saying, but it is hard for me to really hear you when you use words that are disrespectful.
- That is an interesting opinion. Tell me more after class.
- When did you start (feeling, thinking, believing) that? Tell me after class.

Now that you have read these messages, we encourage you to repetitively practice those you might use, or modify them in ways that make them more comfortable for you to say. Notice commonalties among the sentences. They are clear, specific, and brief but to the point and respectful of the other person, even when that person has been disrespectful.

Lowering Shields

Once a power struggle has occurred and a student has developed a hostile attitude, that may be visible or invisible to you. Something must be done to reduce hostility (possibly on the part of both the student *and* teacher). Lowering shields is a technique, borrowed from *Star Trek*, that not only is effective for teachers to use but also to model and teach students to use with others.

The Starship Enterprise raises its shields for defense and protection, but that prohibits communication and robs life support energy. Likewise, people who have their shields up have trouble communicating and existing in comfort in a perceived hostile environment. War is more likely to break out than peace. After an episode where shields are likely to be raised, take time to lower them before trying to teach, communicate, or problem solve. Examples are after an argument, after a student has been removed from the class or school and returns, after implementing an unpleasant consequence, or when a student is angry from an incident with another teacher.

In each of these situations, the teacher is the one who initiates contact. Hopefully the student will learn to initiate contact from a combination of your modeling, this experience, and formal instruction from an experienced adult. Once contact is initiated, the teacher as warmly as is genuinely possible says words similar to: "You and I had a bad time (yesterday, a few minutes ago, just now). I know it made you feel (angry, upset, unhappy, sad, hostile). I feel _____ myself. But I am truly glad you are (still here, back), and I want to start fresh. We both can make each other's day a little better. I'd like to do that for you, and I hope you are willing to help me. How about it?"

Follow with an outstretched hand, a high five, or a hug in a way that lets the student accept or reject your opening.

If the student accepts, then thank him or her and go back to normal activities. If the student rejects, then say, "You don't have to decide now. I'll do my part and start fresh with you. If you decide to start fresh with me, then let me know. I won't hold it against you if you decide you won't." Then return to normal activities.

When you use the Lowering Shields strategy, always do it privately. Be genuine. Never use words or make promises or offers that you do not believe in. Use Lowering Shields to restore harmony, not as a cover for mismanagement of ineffective consequences. It is a communication, not a manipulation. Do not force the student to accept your invitation and do not be personally offended if the student rejects. Often it takes students two or more incidents before enough trust is built to break through the shields, especially if the student has been attacked after lowering his shields in the past by other adults.

Questions and Suggestions on Defusing

To help you identify when to use defusing strategies and which one(s) to choose, reflect upon the following questions and suggestions:

1. We all have things that get to us. What are some things that students do or say that you find irritating?

2. Why do you think they do these things? What basic needs do you think they are trying to meet within themselves that motivate the irritating behaviors? Most problem behavior is sustained by one of these basic needs: belonging (everyone else does it); competence (hiding worries of intellectual inadequacy behind socially inappropriate behavior); power (control or influence); virtue (relative presence or absence of empathy); fun or stimulation.

3. What are you currently doing when students say or do irritating things?

4. Are your current behaviors effectively solving the problems?

5. What strategies can you identify that may be effective in meeting the basic needs that you think are responsible for the problem behavior?

6. Which sentences or strategies in this chapter do you think are applicable to the situation?

You Can Help Us

"I think high schools with a lot of problems, should have surveillance cameras and metal detectors. Metal detectors would help with guns and knives in the school. The surveillance cameras would help with drugs and drug dealing. If the students knew they were being watched, they would be more unlikely to bring these things to school."

— A female student

7. Pick a few of these sentences or strategies and practice them. At first, approach this task as an actor might approach new lines. Don't expect proficiency, and recognize that the final script will be different from the one you are currently rehearsing. Allow yourself the freedom to experiment with the unfamiliar, which will likely make you feel awkward and silly at first. Keep experimenting until you become comfortable with a defusing strategy.

8. Implement one or more defusing strategies when the problem next occurs.

Handling Group Behavior

Every educator knows that a discipline problem is harder to handle if it involves a group instead of an individual. When children hang around in gangs or cliques, they behave very differently than when they are alone or even in pairs. The collective study of group behavior is as expansive as it is fascinating. However, no research is necessary to know that students in groups are bolder, more cruel, less controllable, more likely to break rules, and more prone to violence.

Groups, like individuals, need *control* and *dignity*. Control helps them feel they have the ability to determine what happens to them. Dignity conveys that they are worthwhile to themselves and to others. When these needs are threatened, the group becomes aggressive and hostile even faster than an individual would.

The following suggestions apply to all groups within the school, including serious gangs or even small cliques of friends. They include various ways to recognize the needs of the group and to give them control and dignity in positive ways within reasonable limits. In that way the need for the aggression and hostility that lead to violent behavior is reduced.

• **Learning how to behave in a group is an essential life skill.** Students need to learn how to maintain their own integrity and values when they conflict with group norms. They need to learn positive ways to impress others, how to walk away from trouble and still look macho. They need to know how to withdraw from the group when necessary. Schools are a natural setting for teaching these skills because most groups in a child's life develop in school.

It is easy to assume we are meeting this need by teaching group skills such as active listening, leadership, or staying focused during classroom group activities. Students learn a lot about group behavior from cooperative activities, but they don't learn how to say no to the group or when to make their own way. Teaching these skills as a regular ongoing segment of the curriculum is an important component to countering violence.

• **Not all groups spell trouble, no matter what they might look like.** The kid with the shaved head, body piercing, and "Screw Everybody" t-shirt actually might be a friendly clerk from the local ice cream store who just likes to dress like his friends. Three or four kids with a sinister appearance might generate fear, disgust, or mistrust in adults just as the last generation did with long hair and tie-dyed t-shirts.

After the San Francisco Earthquake of 1989, gangs of kids roamed the streets for days, not looking for trouble but searching for elderly and immobile people to see if they needed help, food, supplies, or aid. By assuming the best *in* groups and *from* groups we are more likely to treat them with dignity and without fear. We can communicate both verbally and nonverbally that we trust and respect them. At the least we don't become their targets and at best we make allies who might help us handle other students in violent situations.

• **Show an active interest.** Check in with students from time to time. Ask how and what they are doing in the manner of a curious friend rather than as a suspicious policeman. Even hostile, hard-core gang members respond in positive ways to individuals who show genuine care and respect. The operative word is *genuine*. Showing interest is not the same as being interested, just as showing respect does not mean having respect. All kids, especially those who have been marginalized out of the mainstream, are highly sensitive to phoniness and manipulation. They reject or even punish adults who pretend to care but really are manipulating.

• **Avoid sarcasm, insults, or negative comments about the way students look, talk, or act.** Joking around is fine but don't let friendly teasing go too far. Teasing leads to "counterteasing," and what starts as friendly banter can lead to hurt feelings. Very few adults, let alone kids in groups, have the wherewithal to say, "That remark hurt my feelings. I prefer that you not say that anymore."

• **Notice little (and bigger) nice things students do and compliment them.**

• **Never discipline, criticize, correct, or insult a group member when he or she is within the group.** The resulting humiliation will destroy any chance of cooperation, and the student will feel it necessary to restore his or her image with friends. This usually means retribution, and you will probably lose any goodwill you have established with all of the group members.

• **Join in with the group without joining the group.** There are many ways to share time and activities with various groups to develop ties and promote understanding. We can watch them play if they are on a sports or drama team or have a music group. Sit with them in the lunchroom and eat together, or simply spend a few minutes chatting at the bus stop or parking lot after school.

However, do not go too far and try to become an ersatz group member. Don't assume a greater role than appropriate or try to copy their unique language. Closeness and caring are important within the context of clear boundaries. If you get too close and learn information about an illegal or rule violating activity, they must be aware that you will take steps to stop them or at least report them. Never fall into the trap of playing at undercover, though. Leave that for trained experts.

• **Ask the group for help.** One way of neutralizing the harm groups can do is to get them involved in positive activities. Even hard-core gang members have done community service when asked by those who believe the gang has had something positive to offer. Some gangs have patrolled the boundaries of city high schools to prohibit drug sales. A few gangs in Los Angeles (who prefer to remain anonymous) have had members speak to younger students in school about the danger of joining gangs and the remorse they had in becoming involved.

Many schools have successfully used the "co-opt" method with individuals and less dangerous types of groups by asking them to help solve the very problem they create. Some examples are playground abusers becoming playground monitors, lunchroom violators becoming lunchroom monitors, tough groups helping stop fights, and negative group leaders becoming peer mediators.

Another way to involve groups is to ask their opinions about dealing with group or gang-related school issues. What do they think about reducing vandalism, fighting, thefts, and put-downs?

Finally, there are an infinite number of altruistic possibilities within a school or the greater community (Curwin 1992, Mendler 1992) for groups of students to become involved in. We have observed the most hardened juveniles improve both short- and long-term behavior patterns when encouraged and permitted to be helpful to others who need them. Group members can all benefit from becoming big brothers, tutors, aids, monitors, and instructors.

When providing helping opportunities for groups (as well as individuals) it is preferable to help people, not things. Tutoring a younger student is preferable to sweeping a floor. In the improbable event that there are not enough people to help in your school or community, then pets or small animals, such as gerbils, are still preferable to things.

- **Solve problems or concerns of group members.** Students often seek out students with similar problems or concerns. If a student is doing poorly academically, the likelihood is that his or her friends are too. Recovery depends on forming new relationships or changing the dynamics that sustain already existing ones.

If a student is hanging with a bad crowd, one of the most effective ways to change his or her friends is to solve the problem common to the group or deal with the unifying concern. Teachers and counselors can be especially attuned to both new friends that students make and to new problems and concerns that might lead to new associates. Early intervention is helpful in resolving problems that might lead to joining the wrong crowd.

- **Provide a new focus.** Especially with groups of younger children, it is possible to provide a new focus to change group behavior. Activities such as athletics, music, art, drama, computers, or the volunteering suggested above can replace a negative focus like hanging around, getting into trouble, vandalizing, stealing, or other misbehavior. The school is an excellent facility to provide alternative activities both during school hours and after school.

This suggestion is separate from the worthy practice of inviting individuals within groups to join already existing activities, teams, organizations, or clubs. We suggest that the group as a whole become an organization, team, or club of its own. Having a new, more positive focus goes a long way toward minimizing violent or hostile behavior.

• **Divide turf.** In some settings, gangs seem to control more turf than school authorities. In other settings, the influence of certain popular groups is stronger at determining school culture than the adults. When cultures clash, most students are influenced by those they most admire or fear.

It is impossible to eliminate the influence of groups, but we give ourselves more influence when we let go of issues over which we have little actual control. This involves two preliminary steps: being intelligent enough to know what you cannot control, and knowing what really matters most to the safety and well being of the school.

An impressive example is how a school in a suburb of Boston, Massachusetts, handled a dangerous neighborhood. Students were constantly wearing hats signifying gang colors and affiliation, despite efforts to stop them. Realizing that the only way to stop this behavior was to expel 90 percent of their students, the school met with the toughest gang and negotiated a deal (divided the turf). The school and the gang agreed to the following: The school allowed hats in the hall, lunchroom, and parking lot, but not in classes, provided no fights broke out. The rule would revert back to "no hats" after two fights within three days.

In addition, the gang and school negotiated for them to police the neighborhood and protect the elementary students on the way home. The school gave up nothing it could enforce and gained a great deal in return. A school cannot lose if it gives up what it can never have and gets something it needs in return.

• **Set firm limits.** Some groups appear dangerous and others are dangerous. If we allow our fear to hinder our ability to exert authority, then we stretch the limits for which we hold the group accountable. A dangerous cycle can be created in a short time, as groups become bolder and more confident that they cannot be controlled.

Administrators, counselors, and a solid majority of teachers must overcome their fear and let groups know when they cross the line of what is acceptable. We cannot let fear stop us from insisting on acceptable behavior and enforcing rules when broken. If misbehavior continues, take whatever steps are necessary to see that it stops. Never allow prejudices against the group to determine when or if you see a rule violation, and always use discretion when implementing consequences, choosing the most effective ones for that particular group. And never allow broken rules to be ignored.

• **Discipline individually.** In most instances, it is preferable to discipline individually when a group acts inappropriately. Students are usually more challenging when they are together, feeding off each other and escalating issues. Meeting alone with the group's leaders can be an effective way of being fair while preserving the integrity of the group and its leaders. This type of meeting is often an effective forum in using the power of the group to solve problems it creates.

Teaching Students Alternatives to Violence

S tudents will never do what they have never seen. When it comes to violence, students won't act in nonaggressive ways unless they have learned techniques for controlling and expressing their angry feelings. We believe educators can teach such techniques in school as part of formal instruction or through the discipline process.

The many activities in this chapter cover two main areas: calming anger and solving problems. Frustrated students with poor anger management skills can become explosive when stressed. In the first section, we seek to provide many relaxation-based strategies that you can easily teach your students. The next section offers your students several effective ways to solve problems nonviolently. All the activities can be used in three ways:

• **Teach the activities as part of the school curriculum.**
Admittedly, primary teachers have more flexibility with time than secondary teachers, and they can more easily incorporate the activities into their classes. But these activities can be included in any course of study that all secondary students take, such as health, family living, or civics. If such courses do not already exist, then a special course could be added as either a weekly event, using a shortened day, or as a six-week module. The important point is that students will not use skills

they do not have, and all the punishments and all the get-tough attitudes in the world cannot alter this fact. If you cannot find a way to teach students the skills for handling aggression and hostility, about the only other solution is to accept the resulting violence.

- **Blend activities with the academic curriculum.** We study wars in history, *combustible* chemicals in science, discordant sounds in music, *conflicting* theories of economics, and competing formulas in math. In short, many academic moments focus on the study of dissent and discord. When antiviolence messages and practices become part of the instructional fabric, students are much more apt to experience meaningful connections to academic activities that alone may seem trite. We encourage teachers to find ways to incorporate the activities in this chapter with academic content.

- **Use these activities as part of an ongoing discipline program.** In *Discipline with Dignity*, we advocate "instructional consequences," which are designed to teach students skills that can help prevent future rule violations. Such consequences are very effective for students who do not know how to follow the rules that they violated. For example, if a student uses unacceptable language because that is what he hears most frequently at home, it is more helpful to teach different words and practice using them than to simply send the child home for two days (where more practice of the undesirable behavior is likely). In the same way, violence is the language of aggression outside the school. Faculty and staff members must understand the difference between students who act violently because they want to and those who do it because they do not know how to behave differently.

There are several other things to keep in mind before considering these activities. One important point is that not every teacher will be a natural at teaching antiviolence or self-control programs. We strongly suggest that all teachers who are given this assignment carefully read, try, and role play each activity before teaching students. We believe it is necessary to directly understand and experience the skills you will teach others so that your credibility is enhanced by both knowledge and practice. It is easier to understand and discuss what to do when you are angry than to actually do it in the heat of the moment. Effective instructors must be aware of this gap and understand how to bridge it.

For reasons not entirely clear to us, some members of your school or community might disagree with the idea of the school helping students relax and assume greater control of their emotions. Some people believe that function to be the responsibility of the family. We certainly agree with that perspective, and, in the ideal world, all families would take full responsibility for developing morality in their children. Unfortunately, ours is not an ideal world, and many children are not taught these important skills. Even students with some experience in anger and stress management can benefit from additional instruction.

Some groups have prevented schools from using calming activities on the grounds that they are somehow antireligious. For example, the *Wall Street Journal* reports that a school in Michigan banned breathing exercises due to pressure from some religious devotees (Nazario 1991). The result was an increase in violent behavior. None of the activities in this section has any connection to religion, mysticism, or anything un-Godly. We hope that educators love children enough to teach them practical antitension skills that will maker them safer. And we hope schools have the courage to stand up for what is best for children and society. It is our moral and educational responsibility to teach students skills for living and for staying alive.

The following exercises are written as they would be presented to students. You can use them in any way that works in your situation. Not every skill described in this chapter will work with every student. Age, maturity, experiences, and environment make some skills more appropriate than others for certain students. We have learned from experience that it is difficult to guess what kind of student will benefit from a specific activity. We have seen tough inner-city youths count to 10 backwards rather than fight, and we have seen junior high girls replace angry thoughts with peaceful words when they believed rivals were trying to steal their boyfriends. Rather than determine for you which strategies and activities are appropriate for your students, we suggest you experiment and tailor your group and individualized training to your experiences and judgment.

If an activity is going to be used as part of a plan for dealing with a student who has broken an antiviolence rule, who does the training and which activities are best for that particular student are best resolved by the teacher, principal, a vice-principal for discipline, or a counselor familiar with the student and the program. It is important for whoever does the intervention to remember that the skills taught to the violator should be offered with the hope that they will be used in actual situations. If skills are taught in a hard-nosed way, they will be associated with punishment. Students will see the skills as something to be avoided. Also, if we teach skills with hostility, we do not model anger control. Teach the skills with an inviting, caring attitude that reflects how you want students to behave when they are angry.

Section I: Techniques for Calming Anger

Introduction for Educators

The best way to get students talking meaningfully about violence is to encourage them to look at what they've seen happening close to them. What are the facts? What are their perceptions? Perhaps the easiest place to begin a discussion is to ask students to describe various times when they've been angry and then probe further by asking them what they think are helpful and harmful ways to express anger. Here are some questions to get things started:

1. How many of you have ever lost your temper? (Expect almost everybody to agree.)

2. How many are about to lose their temper right now? (Expect few, if any, to step forward.)

3. If you are not about to lose your temper now, how do you know that?

4. What can you say about how you are breathing, how hot or cool your face feels, what kind of thoughts you are having?

5. When you are tense, uptight, or angry, what can you say about your breathing, your heart rate, your temperature, your thoughts?

6. When you are angry, how good are you at solving problems?

As the issues of violence, aggression, and hostility come into focus, you can introduce students to the activities for controlling stress that are described in this chapter. This chapter is essentially a curriculum of skills that emphasizes self-control and problem solving. The first section contains activities that help students relax while the second section is designed to help students improve their problem-solving skills.

You can present these activities sequentially but we think it is best to mix and match from both sections to best take care of the needs of your students.

All the strategies work well for most children—and adults. Some older children may already be familiar with strategies such as counting, breathing, and self-talk, but for many younger children, these strategies will be an introduction to anger control.

We offer you a way of talking to your students that includes research and our views; however, we encourage you to substitute your own experiences and those of your students as a basis for discussion and exploration. For example, you might use incidents of violence, aggression, or bullying in your classroom, school, or community as the basis for the activities that follow. You could ask students to share perceptions, facts, and fears either in discussion or by collecting written anecdotes and then using their stories to begin work on a particular strategy. The bottom line is that you are the professional, and we merely offer you a set of tools along with directions for use that can be adapted or altered to fit the needs of your group.

Teach and demonstrate each technique in ways that relate it to real life. For example, you can ask students to imagine being in a crowded hall and accidentally bumping another student, who then tries to start a fight. A self-talk strategy (i.e., it's not worth getting into a fight and I don't need the trouble), along with a breathing strategy (taking a few deep breaths while walking away) can be modeled. Other situations might include teasing that gets out of hand, anger over a game, a disagreement, or being falsely accused by someone. You can have students think of their own situations. Ask them to think of potentially dangerous situations during which they think it would be important to find better ways of staying "cool." Let them know that people usually have to practice the strategies several times to be able to really stay cool when bad stuff is happening.

Suggested Classroom Introduction

Look around at our class. For every 28 of your classmates, four will be victims of either their own or somebody else's aggression. Nine of those 28 students think that violence will shorten their lives. That's according to a poll of teens conducted in 1996 by the Rochester Research Group.

A student remarked in the *Rochester Democrat and Chronicle* (1996), "At my school, there are two kids that are in jail—one for rape and the other for murder. . . . I'm apprehensive about going to school, worried I'll be a statistic. There are fights all the time. It really frightens me."

Our school either has metal detectors or the adults are trying to decide whether they are necessary. There are many schools in which police and security guards are as much a part of the school as teachers and books. Even if things haven't gotten that bad, most schools are trying to make sure that they remain safe by creating zero-tolerance policies for violence so that students who do dangerous things are suspended or expelled.

The world, including the school world, has become a more dangerous place, and it is important that you prepare yourself to handle possible violent behavior that may come your way. Naturally, we hope that it will never be necessary, but if trouble knocks on your door, we want you prepared to deal safely and effectively with people who want to give you problems. And if someone makes you angry, we want you to feel confident that you can remain calm so that you can think of a solution that will solve the problem or at least not make things worse.

Some of you walk on dangerous streets to get to school. You see some kids, maybe even younger than you, with knives and guns. Some of you have had people you love hurt or even killed. You worry that if you seem weak, others will pick on you. You know that the usual advice given by adults doesn't always work: "Walk away. Don't pay any attention to the person who is bothering you." You also know that if you start up with the wrong person, you could wind up hurt or worse. It isn't just kids who live in tough neighborhoods that have to be careful. A big middle-school kid who was a bully in a rural part of Pennsylvania was recently killed by a much smaller kid who he kept harassing. Now, the bully is dead and the other kid is probably going to serve a lot of time in prison or at a juvenile delinquent facility for killing him.

Violence is not just physically hurting someone. Violence is also when people attack you with words or damage your property.

I want you to learn a variety of methods to control your anger when people try to make you mad. Keep in mind that change is never easy. Have you ever tried walking home from school a different way? Have you ever sat in someone else's chair at the dinner table? Have you tried to watch less television, read more books, or play video games only on Sunday?

Most people keep doing things that they are used to doing even when those things don't work. But all people can change. It does take time and patience and guts! Next time you can, watch a little kid who is just starting to walk. Notice how she gets up, walks with her arms up, stumbles, falls, and sometimes even cries. But she gets back up and keeps walking until she is so good at it that she will one day walk as well as you or I. Her practicing makes it possible for her to eventually walk well. With the support of your teacher and other students, you can find safe ways to deal with tough situations.

There are two basic ways that I want to teach you so you are more skilled with and therefore safer in possibly violent situations. Each of these ideas has many different strategies or techniques that you can learn and use.

First, it is important to learn how to not let other people's anger make you angry. You have a lot more control over this than you think. There are many things that we can do to make sure that we keep calm when someone is bothering or threatening us or people we love. It is easier to behave angrily by screaming at someone, calling them a name, pushing back, or fighting. But we gain the advantage when we keep ourselves calm by using the most powerful muscle we own: our brain.

Have you ever watched a great professional quarterback? The great ones are always calm under pressure. That's what makes them great and why they win. When they become emotional, they use their feelings to their own advantage, not to their opponent's. They know to focus their emotions to make them stronger willed at achieving what they want, without allowing others to sidetrack them from a winning strategy.

You'll learn specific ways to control your feelings and angry thoughts when other people try to make you mad. You'll learn how to make your mind and body relax. These techniques are called Calming Anger.

Next, you'll learn how to behave with people who are annoying you. I'll show you how to get people off your back safely and effectively. We know that all people get upset when they are annoyed. It's normal to want to hit, name-call, or hurt someone who shows us no respect. We not only want to win, but we want everyone, including the one who annoys us, to know that we have won. But this almost always leads to continuing problems.

To really win, we have to be in control of ourselves and to make smart choices. Bobby Holley, a black belt in martial arts from Philadelphia who is as tough as anyone in an action movie, never has to fight or even wants to. He says, "Real courage is doing the right thing when others might think you are a coward. Courage is what is inside of you that only you know about. It's not what others think about you." That is why adults usually tell students to ignore when someone is bothering them. But we know that ignoring doesn't always work to stop someone who bullies. If being aggressive or ignoring doesn't work, what does? The second group of methods teaches you how to solve problems either by yourself or with other people. Someone who picks on you or wants to start a fight is creating a problem. You need to know how to solve problems and how to remind yourself to use what you know when you feel angry.

It takes self-confidence to do things other than bother people, especially if they bother you first. You will get lots of ideas that will help you realize that each and every one of you is special and important. You will realize that you don't have to blow out someone else's candle to make yours burn brighter. You will learn different ways of solving problems.

There are many easy-to-learn things that make it possible to calm yourself when you are angry. Every one of these methods has been used by young people to relax when they feel angry. But what works for one person may not always work for another. We have preferences for different sports, music, food, and cars. Just as you might try different sports before you decide on your favorites, try each of these exercises several times before you decide which, if any, you will want to use most often. The time to practice and decide what is best to do is before you have a problem.

Counting from 1 to 10

Thomas Jefferson, the third President of the United States, once said that you should first count to 10 before you do anything when you are upset. People have tried this very thing for the last 250 years, and many of them say it works. So, the next time you feel angry, try counting to 10.

In fact, make believe right now that someone just said or did something that makes you mad. Try to picture it as best as you can in your imagination. While you probably won't feel as angry as you would in a real situation, this is a good way to practice. Most people find that it is best to close their eyes while they practice this so that they aren't distracted by outside sights. In real life, you'll probably keep your eyes open when someone is bothering you.

What did you want to say or do to the person who upset you? Now that you are feeling some anger, try counting from 1 to 10. Do this several times.

How did your feelings change after you counted to 10? If not much happened, repeat the exercise as many as 10 more times. The next time someone or something upsets you, you might decide to try this method.

Counting from 10 to 1

Counting backwards from 10 to 1 works the same as the exercise where we counted from 1 to 10. But in this case, you start at 10 and slowly count backwards to 1.

Try it now. Imagine someone or something has upset you. How does that feel? Now, close your eyes and slowly count backwards from 10 to 1. Do this once, or several times—whatever you think you need.

Consider how your feelings changed after you counted down from 10 to 1. The next time you're upset about someone or something, counting like this might be something good for you to try.

Count Backwards by 5 Starting at 100

Counting by 5's to 100 works well with many students from about 6th grade on up. No one can say exactly why it works so well, but it does. Maybe it's because you have to think a little bit, and that slows down anger. Thinking about something that doesn't bother us, like numbers, gives us a few seconds to get our thoughts away from the anger so that we may either settle down or decide what to do next.

To give it a try, picture an aggravating situation. It may help to close your eyes while you picture this. Once you're feeling some anger, count by 5's to 100. How does this method work for you? Is it different from simply counting from 1 to 10 or 10 to 1? The next time you're angry or upset, you may want to try this out.

Deep Breathing

One of the best and easiest ways to relax is to take some deep breaths. Just breathe in deeply through your nose (or mouth if that's more comfortable), and let the air travel all the way deep into your chest. Then breathe out slowly. Repeat this several times. This is especially good to do when you feel uptight or angry.

An alternative is to take in big, deep breaths, then each time you breathe out, imagine you're breathing like a fiery dragon.

You can stay calm a lot longer if you do this kind of breathing over and over for approximately three to five minutes. That sounds like a long time, but it's well worth a try!

Deep Breathing and Counting Together

Several years ago, a man named Dr. Benson discovered a simple method that helps many people feel relaxed. He was a medical doctor who was curious and doubtful about claims of better health made by some nondoctors who believed that meditation helped cure people of a variety of medical problems thought to be caused by stress. To his surprise, Dr. Benson (1976) found that meditation did help people feel relaxed and that it helped several people to actually lower their blood pressure. High blood pressure can be one symptom of stress. Even better, he found that a simple breathing and counting exercise worked just as well to help people relax and lower their blood pressure.

As a student, you can benefit from learning this breathing and counting method as another way of keeping yourself calm. Dr. Benson advises doing this activity twice a day for 10 minutes each time. If you often get angry or if you get angry very quickly, it is a good idea for you to follow this advice because this exercise can help you stay calmer when things that usually get you upset are happening.

Just breathe in deeply through your nose (or mouth), and as you breathe out, silently say the number one. Keep doing this several times. Once again, breathe in slowly and deeply all the way down to your stomach. As you breathe out, say the number one. You should do this for at least several minutes if you really want to relax. But if your goal is simply to release some anger quickly, you can just do this for a couple of minutes. Even just a couple of times can help.

Let's try it now and see how it can even work when you are upset or angry. Imagine a situation that would make you angry. When you're feeling a little tense, breathe in slowly and deeply, all the way to your chest. As you breathe out, silently say the number one. Do this as many times as it takes for you to feel less upset.

Count by 5's and Breathe

This is similar to the exercise where you say "one" while breathing in and out. But in this exercise, you actually count while you breathe in, and you count while you breathe out.

Close your eyes and silently count to five while you breathe in. Then hold your breath and count to five. Now, breathe out to the count of five.

So, this exercise goes: IN 2 3 4 5, HOLD BREATH 2 3 4 5, OUT 2 3 4 5. Do this at least 10 times if you want to relax, or three times if you just want to do something other than hurt someone by getting angry with them.

Use Calming Words

Instead of counting, many students have found that they can calm themselves down by silently saying words that make them feel better. Even better is combining breathing and calming words. Like most of these activities, this technique works best when practiced with your eyes closed.

For example, try the following. While you inhale through your nose or mouth, silently say the word CALM. When you exhale, silently say the word DOWN. Do this several times. You are telling and teaching yourself to calm down, which is really good advice when things get hot. Most students notice that doing this really helps. Other words or phrases that might have the same effect:

- Chill Out
- Relax (Re . . . lax)
- In Charge
- Be Cool
- Stay Cool
- Happy (Hap . . . py)
- I'm Cool

Other words might work better for you. You can try any that you'd like. Just close your eyes (or keep them open if you must) and in the privacy of your own thoughts, say one word as you breathe in and another as you breathe out.

Letting Go

Note to Teacher: This strategy is best used one-on-one with a student in a counseling situation when he or she has behaved violently or seems ready to explode. A counselor, teacher, or administrator can guide the exercise, depending on who the student trusts the most.

Take an empty chair and put it in front of you. Imagine that someone you feel like slugging is sitting in that chair. Tell that person all of the things that he or she is doing that make you angry. Say anything and everything you want. Don't hold back.

If you feel anger in your fists, take a soft pillow and put it on the chair. While you are imagining that the person at whom you are angry is there, let yourself hit the pillow as if the person is really there. You also might want to tell the person how you feel in words or grunts as you hit the pillow.

Remember that there is nothing wrong with how you feel. Everyone gets angry from time to time. Sometimes other people do things that really get us mad. When this happens, we have to try not to do things we'll regret later.

A 13-year-old boy was locked up because he killed his brother with a gun. Before that happened, he was just a regular kid who had friends, listened to music, liked to play ball, and did okay at school. His brother had been irritating him for a while about things, calling him names, and trying to be better than he was.

In a fit of anger, this boy loaded a rifle in the house and shot his brother three times. He felt terrible after he did this. He even covered his brother with a blanket, forgetting that it was no longer necessary to keep him warm. He wound up at a youth detention center where he felt badly every day for having killed his brother. At one point he said, "I would do anything to get my brother back." But he couldn't!

It is so important that we find safe ways to express our angry feelings. It is never wrong to feel anger or fear or even like killing someone. It is only wrong to do these things. Take care of things before you lose your cool!

Scream It Out

Note to Teacher: While this exercise shows students how to safely let off steam, it's also great fun to practice in class—especially for young students. You might practice this as a transition from high-energy, boisterous situations to those that require quiet and calm. This activity also is effective to practice in one-on-one settings as described above.

When you are really upset and you want to let someone else have it, put a pillow over your face and scream into it. Nobody will hear you, and you will probably feel better. You also might pound the pillow after you have finished screaming. Finally, use one of the breathing or counting strategies you have learned and do it at least five times. Notice how much better you feel after you relieve your tension in this way.

Feel It Out

At times, people feel tense and don't know why. We just aren't sure why we feel bad or mad or upset or sad. Maybe it is because of a lot of little things. Maybe someone important to you just said or did something that disappointed you, but you just don't feel comfortable telling him or her. When these things happen, you can still use many of the techniques you have learned. Sometimes it helps to just talk it out.

Many students talk to themselves out loud as if another person was there. It can help get a lot off your chest. But if that won't work, then maybe you are just in the mood to be loud or even cry. Most people feel better after they have released their feelings. You actually practice saying or doing what you want without anybody else there. Then you can decide about whether you want to do something more, such as really tell someone how you feel. But, by doing it this way, without anybody else around, you don't have to be concerned about how they might react. And many times it is best to calm yourself without getting directly involved with someone else so that you don't make matters worse.

Working Out

When we feel angry, our muscles usually get angry, too. We may grit our teeth, clench our fists, frown, or stomp our feet. Our muscles can make us strong, or they can get us into trouble if we use them the wrong way. Fights are done with muscles, so is pulling the trigger on a gun, and so are many games we play. We use our mouth muscles to talk trash or to smile, and our leg muscles to kick, walk, or run.

When you are angry, it is useful to help your muscles let off steam so that they won't get you into trouble. Some of the things that you can do are lift weights, run, ride a bike, and hit or kick a heavy punching bag. Some people like to do aerobic exercises. Make a plan about what you will do when you get angry enough to get physical with other people.

Try to remember that when we are really mad it is normal to feel like hurting someone. But almost all the kids that I have talked with who have hurt someone or even killed someone feel really bad about what they did afterwards and sometimes there is just no way to make it better. Do things before you get into trouble.

Relax Your Whole Body

Relaxing your whole body is another thing to do when you want to "chill."

First, sit up straight in a comfortable chair with your hands in your lap and your feet on the floor. Be away from everyone. Close your eyes.

Next, tense or tighten or squeeze the muscles in your feet, legs, and toes as tightly as you can. Silently count to five as you hold this position. Then release and stretch out those muscles.

Now go to the muscles of your chest and stomach. Tighten up those muscles as you silently count to five, then relax.

Go to your arms, fingers, and shoulders. Tighten up these muscles. Silently count to five, then let go. Feel the relaxation.

Now go to your head and neck. Scrunch up the muscles of your face as you count to five, then relax those muscles. Do it again and make sure that you scrunch your mouth, nose, eyes, and teeth, and then relax each of those parts of your body.

Now go back to your feet and do all of your body again. Squeeze or tighten each body part, count to five, then relax. When you finish, open your eyes and notice how relaxed your whole body feels.

Make Mental Movies

Suppose that someone has just said or done something that really bothers you. Or maybe something bad happened and you couldn't control it. You're so upset that you feel like going off. You don't want to because you know bad stuff is going to happen and you don't need the grief. To make yourself feel better, try making a movie in your mind. Here's how.

First, imagine that you are in a movie theater and you are the only one there. The movie has yet to start. You are looking at a blank screen. Very slowly you notice the movie is beginning—but in a strange way. The thing that is annoying you is beginning to come onto the screen from the left side. Notice all there is to see, hear, and feel about the people or things that are bothering you.

Just as you start getting mad again, the movie picture begins to fade. It moves off the screen to the right until it gets harder and harder to see. The movie ends and is replaced again by a blank screen. As you keep looking, you notice that another movie begins to move onto the screen from the left. As it becomes more clear, you notice that it is a place you love to be, with people and things you enjoy. Watch it closely. Notice the colors, hear the sounds, watch the action, smell the smells. Now imagine that you actually step into the picture and become an actor in the movie. You are actually in the movie.

Maybe you are at the beach listening to the waves. Possibly you are walking in the mountains watching the sky and feeling the brisk, clean air. Maybe you're just hanging out at your favorite place with your favorite people eating your favorite food. Stay here and enjoy the scene for just another moment.

Now leave the movie and return to your seat in the theater. As you are now watching, begin to notice the picture fading out to the left as before. This time, take along the memories of the movie as you sit for a final moment before leaving and getting on with your life.

Make It Ridiculous

You don't and can't control all the things that happen to you, but you can control how you react to those things. Imagine someone just called your mother an ugly name. Instead of getting angry right away, pretend that the person who just said this is 2-years-old, wearing a pink bow in her hair, and has her thumb in her mouth. Isn't that ridiculous? Of course it is. Can you see how you would immediately feel differently if you approached the situation that way?

There are other ways to make a problem situation ridiculous so that you laugh rather than react with anger. Pretend that the person using the put-down:

- has ink running down his mouth as he's talking,
- is missing his brain,
- has her shoes on backwards, or
- is singing the put-down while playing circus music.

Do you get the idea? Maybe you and your friends can add to this list and then use it when necessary. For example, let's think of as many silly pictures or other images as we can, and then see the people who usually do things that bother us now doing those same things in the silly picture. Let's say that someone is calling me a name but their tongue is upside down, or someone is pushing me but their hands are made of feathers. After coming up with these images, practice using them while you are picturing a tense situation.

Use Personally Spiritual Images or Thoughts

Note to Teacher: Bringing spirituality or religion into the classroom can be controversial, and certain practices have been declared illegal. Many people have strong feelings and opinions on both sides of the issue. Each educator, school, and community needs to grapple with issues that have no easy answers. While religious beliefs can be a source of divisiveness and even war, strong spiritual beliefs can sustain a person during times of stress. We believe that a lack of spiritual connection is related to problems of violence and aggression, so we advocate the use of spiritually uplifting images, icons, and thoughts as a means to helping students daily connect with this component of who they are.

Nearly three out of every four people in the United States say they belong to one religion or another (National Ethos Survey 1996). In the United States, all people have the right to practice their religion without forcing other people to believe the same things. Having religious thoughts can be a very relaxing and reassuring thing for a lot of people. Even people who are not religious can sometimes enjoy spiritual thoughts, which can help them make good decisions.

For example, if you believe in God, it might be a good idea to ask

yourself what God would think of your actions before you act. Would
He approve? Would He think of you as a strong person? Would He
consider your acts to be kind, generous, or loving? If you do not
believe in God, how do you feel about the Golden Rule: Treat others
as you wish to be treated?

Now just suppose that you want to use your spiritual or religious
beliefs to help you relax or to like yourself more or to be reminded
about doing the right thing. Try doing the following.

While sitting, lying down, daydreaming, or exercising, think a spiritual message several times. You can even coordinate the message with
your breathing as you did in earlier exercises. As you inhale (breathe
in) think the words I LOVE and as you exhale (breathe out) say the
name of a spiritually important image (such as God, Jesus, Torah,
Allah, Buddha). If you do not believe in or belong to an organized
religion, say "I" when you breathe in and "love" when you breathe
out, or "Be" (inhale deeply) . . . (exhale in a long breath) "kind."
Repeat the exercise several times.

Section II: Techniques for Solving Problems

Suggested Classroom Introduction

Problem-solving strategies provide ways for us to act effectively
without doing damage to ourselves or others. Along with calming
ourselves when angry, we need to be good at figuring out how to
solve problems we have or that others try to give us. If we let other
people give us their solutions, then they have power over us.
Sometimes that can be good—such as when a teacher or parent shares
with you knowledge they have learned because they care about you.
But each of us has the power to make our own decisions and we need
to decide who we will allow to influence us and who we won't.
Otherwise, others will control what we do and what happens to us.
For example, if someone wants to get you into trouble and uses a put-
down, you slam them, get caught, and then get into trouble, the other
person learns quickly that he has power over you. If I can get you to
do anything I want because you want to join my gang, then you have
given me your power.

We'll be learning about techniques that will help you get better at solving problems in a lot of ways, including how to stay in control of deciding who has the power in your life. Let's look at some of these possibilities.

The Six-Step Solution

Note to Teacher: This six-step procedure can be learned and practiced by all students to give them an effective way of dealing with problem situations before they do something hurtful to themselves or others. The six steps are: (1) Stop and calm down, (2) Think, (3) Decide, (4) Choose a back-up solution in case the first one doesn't work, (5) Act, (6) Evaluate.

Good teaching that is motivating gives meaning to the content. Meaning for this and most activities in this section can be defined in collaboration with the class. Brainstorm a variety of social and interpersonal problem situations with your class and then use the steps of this strategy to find solutions. After teaching the six-step solution, you might want to make a chart with the steps and hang it in the classroom. You'll also note that there are several questions to ask students in steps 2, 3, and 6. You could have a master chart of the six steps and then individual charts that list the steps along with relevant questions to write beneath each. In this way, students can look at visual reminders while they are learning and internalizing these processes. Younger children might enjoy making art projects of each step.

Step 1: Stop and calm down. Before we do anything that we may feel sorry about later, the first thing to do is stop. Do nothing. There is always time to act on your first impulse later if that is what you really want to do.

First, pay attention to the signs that your body gives you when it feels tense. You might notice that your teeth or fists are clenched, you may have trouble swallowing, you may feel hot, or you may be sweating. You might notice that you feel like exploding.

When these things happen, take a deep breath and picture a big red light or stop sign in front of you. Pay attention to this. Do not do anything except stop. That will give you time to decide if the best thing is to explode or to do something else.

After you stop, it is now time to calm down. Doing more breathing or counting exercises or any of the strategies we learned about calming anger can really help.

Step 2: Think. Now that you have calmed down some, it is time to think! You need to decide what to do and what will happen if you do it. The ability to do these last two things is what really makes us different and special from other animals. When animals are upset or under pressure, then they will either fight or run away. People want to do those same things, and at times there are no better choices. But unlike other animals, you can think and decide. After you think and decide, you may still decide to run or fight! But at least you will have done so after considering all of the good and bad things that can happen. And you will mostly find that there are far better choices that let you win without getting into trouble or hurting other people. Remember that winning requires calm under pressure, and making choices that give you control.

A very interesting thing happens every time you think about doing something. It gives you a chance to do something else! For example, if you are feeling mad because someone just called your mother a name and you get angry, that mad feeling may lead you to think, "I'll bust his face!" But as soon as you have that thought, you have a chance to do something else *because you haven't done it yet.* So the idea is to first stop and calm down, then think before you decide and act.

Good thinking always begins with good questions. It is important to see how the questions we ask ourselves lead to the decisions we want to have happen to us. Be in control or in charge of what you do; don't put someone else in charge. Here are some good questions to ask right after you stop and calm down. You don't need to ask yourself all these questions, but it helps to know them all so you can use the best ones for whatever situation you are in.

- Why am I feeling so mad?
- Did I do anything that might have annoyed or offended the other person and might have caused his reaction? If so, what did I do?
- How does the other person feel?
- What is my problem?
- Who could I talk to about the problem before I do anything?
- Have I ever felt this way before?
- What did I do before to try and solve a similar problem?
- How did it work out?

Step 3: Decide. Now that you have done some good thinking, it is time to make a decision. In making a decision, the two most important things to consider are:

- What do I want to happen?
- What will happen if I actually do what I think?

The first question asks that you choose a goal. All successful people have a goal. This tells them what they want to achieve and when to feel proud at their accomplishment. Goals are things like:

- I will do my homework for one hour.
- I will read two books and finish my book report two days before it is due.
- I will use the word please when I ask for something.
- I will use words rather than fists when I feel mad.

The second question asks you to think about the consequences of what you do before you do it. For example, let's say that someone has just challenged you to a fight. After you stop and calm down, and think using the questions above, it is time to decide on a goal. Let's say your goal is: The person will stop calling me names. You now need to decide how you will meet the goal. So it is time to brainstorm all the ideas you can think of that might solve this problem. At first, don't even concern yourself with whether or not a solution will work. It is most important that you come up with as many possible solutions as you can. In this case, some of the solutions may be:

- I'll punch him in the face.
- I'll call his mother a name.
- I'll get my friends after him.
- I'll tell him to shut up.
- I'll tell him I don't like what he said.
- I'll look him in the eye, say nothing, and walk away.

Each solution has consequences. So it is important that you predict the consequences before you act. Questions to ask yourself are:

- Will the solution solve the problem?
- If I do the solution, what might the other person do?
- Is the solution against the rules?
- What will other important people in my life do if I do the solution?

• Am I willing to accept the consequences of the solution?

Let's say Joe decides to punch Pete after Pete calls Joe's mother a name. Joe's goal is to do something that gets Pete to stop while at the same time he stands up to Pete so he doesn't look weak. Joe thinks, "I'll punch him in the face!" He quickly realizes that this solution might solve the problem because he won't look weak, but he also knows that Pete's pretty tough and might punch him back harder. He also knows that punching is against the rules and will likely lead to a suspension from school. Also, Miss Lanier, his guidance counselor, probably will feel disappointed if he gets into trouble again. Joe decides that Pete isn't worth the trouble, so he considers other options, such as walking away, telling someone, writing a note, or saying what he thinks to Pete. But he's not sure, so he decides to do nothing, at least until tomorrow.

Step 4: Decide on another solution in case the first one doesn't work. Every sports team starts a game with a plan to beat the other team. If the plan works, they stay with it. But every good coach knows that the plan may not work as well in the game as it did in practice. So before the game is even played, he and the team have a back-up plan to use just in case. Just like a good coach, you need to have at least one more possible solution ready in case the first one doesn't work. You are your own coach!

Step 5: Act. Once you stop and calm down, and think and decide before doing anything, you have taken control of the situation. You are now in charge of what happens to you. So it is now time to act. You simply carry out your decision and see if it works. You'll know it works if it meets your goal.

For example, when Joe decides to walk away, he will soon know whether or not Pete stops or continues his put-downs. If he stops, then the solution definitely worked. If he doesn't, then Joe either needs to give the solution more time to work or he needs to try a different solution. Some situations demand immediate action, and you'll want one or two solutions to use right away. If you have a recurring problem, you might want to try your first solution three or four times. If it's not working, then try another solution.

Step 6: Evaluate. The final three questions to ask in using this method are:

- Did I reach my goal?
- If the same problem happens again, what will I do?
- Are there any people I can think of (parents, friends, teacher) who might help me figure out how to best make my solution work or to help me think of another that might work better?

Practice the Method: Sally is in the cafeteria when she sees Lois and Joyce laughing while they are looking at her. They come closer and Lois says, "Where'd you get those clothes—at the Goodwill?" Both Lois and Joyce laugh even harder, and some of the other kids who are sitting nearby hear this also. Sally is embarrassed but doesn't know what to do. You are Sally's friend, and you want to help her deal with this situation. Help her decide on a solution by using the steps in the strategy above.

Figure 4.1
TECHNIQUES FOR SOLVING PROBLEMS
THE SIX-STEP SOLUTION

1. **Stop and calm down.**
   Pay attention to the signs that your body gives you when it feels tense.

2. **Think.**
   Consider your options. Think about the many different actions you can choose to take.

3. **Decide.**
   Choose a goal: What do you want to happen?
   Think about the consequences: What will happen if you actually do what you are thinking?

4. **Choose a second solution, in case the first solution doesn't work.**
   Always have a back-up plan ready.

5. **Act.**
   Carry out your decision.

6. **Evaluate.**
   Did you reach your goal?
   If the same problem occurs again, what will you do?
   Are there any people (parents, friends, teacher) who might help you as you figure out the best solutions?

Meeting a Goal

Goals are things that we want to achieve. We reach a goal by making a plan. If you're building a model airplane, directions help you assemble the model in the most precise way. In the same way, a good plan helps you achieve your personal goals. Setting goals helps you know when you have accomplished something of value. Here is how to create a good goal (adapted from Mendler 1990).

- Decide on a goal you want to reach and say it. For example, "When someone bumps into me I want to either walk away or say how I feel. I don't want to fight because I have decided that it isn't worth it. My goal is . . ."
- Decide on a plan you need to get you there. In other words, what are the steps you need to take in order to meet your goal? For example, "First, I'll walk far enough away so that I probably won't bump into anyone. But if I do or they bump into me, I'll say excuse me. If that isn't enough, I'll tell them I didn't mean anything by it—it was just an accident. If that still doesn't work, I'll tell them that getting into a fight isn't worth the hassle to you and then I'll walk away."
- Check your plan with a parent, teacher, or trusted friend.
- Do each step in your plan, one at a time.
- Reward yourself when you have reached your goal. Think about the things you enjoy, such as listening to music, getting clothes, telling yourself you did a good job, sharing your success by telling someone special about it, or taking a bike ride. Pick something after you have accomplished your goal, and treat yourself to a job well done. You might even want to make a list of possible rewards and add to the list as you find new things. Keep the list handy so that you can have an easy way to remind yourself that your behavior has earned a reward.

Figure 4.2 summarizes this strategy.

Things I Control, Things I Don't

It is important to know the difference between problems that you can solve and problems that you can't. It is not always easy to tell the difference, but some things are more obvious than others. You can control which television show you watch or which friend you call. You can't control whether the television works or if your friend is interested in hanging out.

Figure 4.2
MEETING A GOAL

1. What is your goal?
   My goal is _____.

2. What is my plan to achieve my goal?
   I will_____.
   I will_____.

3. What will I do if my plan doesn't work?
   I will_____.
   I will_____.
   I will not_____.

4. With whom will you check your plan?

   _____

   _____

5. What reward(s) will I give myself when I have done all I can to achieve my goal? (Tip: Sometimes you can do everything right but things don't work out as you wish. You can still feel proud of your effort!)

Some problems can be completely controlled while others cannot. We cannot control a parent's drinking problem, mom and dad's decision to divorce, or a father's choice to have no relationship with his child. We don't control the neighborhood we live in or how much money our mother gets for child support. We don't decide when an adult chooses to touch or abuse our private parts. The idea is to figure out the problems in your life over which you have some or complete control and those over which you have none. Then, you can do something to solve the problems that can be solved and decide how to make the best of situations over which you have little control. By looking at things this way, no problem grows so big that you allow it to take over your life.

First, write down the things in your life that make you angry. Nobody will see what you write, but if you worry that someone might peek, then just write a word or a symbol that only you know.

Next, put a "C" next to those things over which you have a lot of control. Then, put an "N" next to those things over which you have no control. If you aren't sure, you might check with a trusted friend, teacher, counselor, or parent to get their opinion.

Next, set goals and develop plans to deal with those things over which you have control For example, "I want to have more contact with my father (goal) so I will call him (plan)."

Decide what you will do if your plan doesn't work. For example, "I called my father, and he promised again to pick me up for a visit but never came. He often lets me down. I'm going to invite him at least two more times for a visit, and if he doesn't come, I'm going to remind myself that he has a lot of problems and that I am still loved by my mother and grandmother." It can be helpful to figure this out with a trusted other person like a friend, parent, neighbor, or teacher. Sometimes a school psychologist or social worker can help because they've received special training for helping students with problems and questions that can be very difficult to face all alone.

For the things on your list that have an "N" beside them, your challenge is to figure out how not to let them bother you as much as they are now. For example, "I can't control that drugs are sold on the street corner and that lots of kids are shooting guns in the street. I can control my decision to do drugs or not, when I walk on the street, and what I should do if I hear gunshots while I'm outside."

Practice the Method: Read the following situation and then answer the questions:

Jamil gets into fights at school. When that happens, he gets suspended. Some kids make fun of his clothes. Whenever someone calls him a name or says something nasty about his family, he gets right into it with them by either calling them a name or by hitting. Jamil's father almost never sees him, and he misses him a lot but doesn't tell anyone how he feels because he is embarrassed that his father really has nothing to do with him. A few older kids have tried to get Jamil to join their gang, and he is thinking about doing just that. The kids are nice to him, they seem to have fun hanging out with each other, and Jamil is pretty lonely. His mom tries to get him to do his homework and talks to him about how important it is to do well in school. But Jamil often doesn't do his homework and says that he is bored at school. He doesn't like his teacher and she gets angry with him a lot because she thinks he doesn't "try."

Questions

1. Does Jamil have any control over what his father does?

2. What do you think about his anger at other kids who call him names?

3. Are they worth the hassle of Jamil getting suspended from school?

4. How do you think Jamil really feels about his father?

5. It's tough on kids when their parents don't treat them right. Do you think that any of Jamil's anger that he gives to other kids really belongs to his father?

6. What can Jamil do about his sadness that his father doesn't care so that he doesn't hurt himself by failing or by hurting others?

7. List all the things that Jamil has at least some control over. Can he decide to do his homework? Join or not join the gang? Find other friends? Get help from anyone at school?

Solving My Problems

Here is another way to solve a problem. First, name the problem. Be specific in saying out loud what the problem is. It is not enough to say things like, "She's unfair!", "He doesn't like me!", "She's always getting on my case for no reason!" Those are too general. It is better to say, "She yells at me when she thinks I haven't worked hard enough." Or, "He bugs me when he thinks I'm bugging my little brother." Or, "The teacher and principal gave me detention because they saw me push another kid."

Next, name what you want to have happen. This is your goal. It may be something like, "I want the teacher to understand that math is hard for me, and even when I work hard, I still usually don't understand." Or, "I want Mom to realize that my little brother doesn't listen when I talk and that I need to bug him to get rid of him." Or, "I want the teacher and principal to be more fair by knowing that the kid I pushed actually pushed me first."

Now, say what you will do. This is your plan. It may sound like, "I will tell the teacher that I need extra help because math is not my best subject." Or, "I'll go to my room and lock the door when I need to not be bothered by my brother." Or, "I'll remind myself that pushing is against the rules even if I'm pushed first and that getting into trouble isn't worth it."

Now, say what you will do if your plan doesn't work. This is your back-up plan. For example, "If the teacher doesn't give me extra help, I'll ask a friend or another teacher." Or, "If the lock on my door is broken or my brother keeps banging, I'll tell Mom." Or, "If the kid keeps pushing me, I'll ask him to stop, then tell him to stop, and then finally tell whoever is in charge."

Next, say your plan and back-up plan to someone you trust and respect for their feedback. If there is nobody you choose to tell, ask yourself how you think someone you respect who usually solves problems peacefully would handle the situation.

Now it's time to carry out your plan. It is important that you do your plan at least three times. If things still don't work out, then try the back-up plan at least three times. If that doesn't work, then talk it over to see if you can borrow an idea from someone you trust that may work better. So, if necessary, the final step in all of this is to change the plan.

Learning to Have Patience

All babies expect to have their needs met immediately. When they are hungry, they cry and expect to be fed. If they aren't fed, they keep crying. It is normal for them to be fed right away and totally sensible for them to get angry or scream if that doesn't happen.

As we grow and mature, we must learn that we won't always have our needs met right away. We must learn that we cannot always eat or use the toilet the instant we feel the urge. Unless we learn this skill, we are doomed to feel frustrated or angry at other people for not giving us what we think we are entitled to get. We may feel jealous of other people who have what we want or think we deserve. We must be willing to work for what we want and learn to accept that sometimes we'll get it and sometimes we won't.

Learning patience means practicing not getting what you want without feeling frustrated and angry. Some things to practice:

- Show up to class on time if you're often late.
- Say good morning to a teacher you don't like.

- Walk away from someone trying to pick a fight.
- Wait to go to the bathroom for several minutes after you first feel you have to.
- Wait in line with a smile and positive thoughts.
- Raise your hand to be recognized.
- Keep your cool when you think an adult in charge is unfair.
- Work for 10 more minutes than usual on something you don't like.
- Work for 20 more minutes than usual on something you don't like.
- Work for 10 more minutes on something that you do like to make sure it is as good as you can possibly make it.
- Walk away if someone bumps you in the hall.
- Keep calm when someone cuts in front of you in line.

Question: What situations have you seen that are good examples of times when students need to learn and practice patience?

Learning patience doesn't happen overnight and it can be helpful when others appreciate the efforts we make to sacrifice things we want

---

Figure 4.3
SOLVING MY PROBLEMS: A PLAN

1. Name the problem.
2. Name what you want to have happen.
3. Decide what you will do.
   This is your plan.
4. Decide what you will do if your plan doesn't work.
   This is your back-up plan.
5. Tell your plan and back-up plan to someone you trust and respect. Get their feedback. If you choose to tell no one, ask yourself how someone you respect who usually solves problems peacefully would handle the situation.
6. Carry out your plan.
7. If necessary, change the plan.

right away. Try noticing and appreciating other students or adults
when you see them acting in a patient way. It can also help to keep a
"Patience Journal" in which you write down or draw instances during
the day when you wanted something right away but stayed calm and
acted respectfully when it didn't work out.

The Invisible Shield or Bulletproof Vest

Imagine owning a shield of steel armor or a bulletproof vest. When
you have it on, nothing can penetrate it. The protection is so tough
that swords bend and bullets ricochet. To be successful and nonviolent
in the real world, each of us needs to build our own mental shield or
vest. This kind of shield costs no money, and we can control when to
use it. To create it, all you need to do is follow some basic guidelines.

First, recognize when someone is mentally attacking you. This is
fairly easy to do. You know when someone is saying hurtful words,
someone is in your face, or someone is talking about you with others.
Can you think of any other hurtful things that people do which make
you feel mad? Be as specific as you possibly can be.

Next, picture your shield or bulletproof vest. Before you do anything about what is being said to or about you, picture putting on
your shield or vest. What does it look like? If you had to draw it,
could you? If not, keep working at it. It might even help to look at a
book of ancient weapons to get some ideas for shields.

Now that you are wearing your shield or vest, imagine that the
attacker's words or looks are stopped by the vest or bent by the shield.
You cannot be hurt as long as you are wearing the protection. Enjoy
knowing that only you can see and feel the vest or shield. You can
choose who you tell about it and who you don't.

Words That Work

Your invisible shield keeps you from being hurt during an attack,
but you may need additional defenses if your opponents don't give up
easily. So we have developed defenses that stop someone's attack without damaging them. The whole idea is to stop violence by not getting
suckered into continuing it. For example, someone calls your mother a
nasty name, determined to bait you into a fight. If you get into the
fight (with your fists or words), chances are things will only get worse:
the police get called, you get suspended, you get punished at home.

Was it worth it? Maybe you think it was, but do you think that your mother would agree if you wound up hurt or dead?

Instead of fighting, you can learn to use safe words that will stop almost all attackers from continuing. At first, they will seem weird. You'll probably think that there is no way you could use these words because they aren't the real you. But with practice and discipline, you can keep others from robbing you of your self-control. Not all of the words will work all the time. But the more sentences you learn to use, the better prepared you will be to deal with the attack.

• **Use "I" Sentences.** These are sentences that tell how you feel, what you want, and what you will do. They begin with the words "when you." Then they tell the person how you feel: "I feel." They end with telling the person what you want, expect, or will do. So there are three parts to an I-sentence:

When you (say or do) _____,
I feel_____, and (or but)
(I want or will)_____.

For example, Jack takes Nancy's books. She says, "When you take my books I feel angry and don't want to be friends. I want my books back now."

Jose is bugged by Luis and Rolando to join their gang. He says, "When you ask me to join the gang, I feel honored because I know you think I'm tough. But I'm just interested in being friends with you guys."

Leo has just called Mitch's mom a nasty name. Mitch looks sternly at Leo and says, "When you call my mother that, I get real upset and feel like busting you up. But getting into trouble isn't worth it so I'm gonna walk away."

Let's give this a try. Imagine that someone is trying to get you into trouble. They either said or did something that you don't like. Try to put together and then use an I-Sentence.

• **Be Polite.** It occasionally works to use the word "please" as a way of getting someone to stop bugging you. For example, "Please give me my book back," or, "Please watch out, I don't like getting bumped."

• **Agree with the Put-Down.** This requires a lot of self-confidence, but it can be one of the most effective things to do in order to get someone to stop hassling, nagging, or bugging you. All you have to do is learn to calmly agree with what the other person says. That is not easy because it is normal to feel angry and want to attack back. But it really isn't worth it, and when you attack back, you just wind up giving the person who bugged you what he or she wanted: your power. After all, he or she was trying to get you mad, and by getting mad you are giving that person the control he or she wants. That just makes no sense.

Expect to practice this several times before you are ready to do this. You have to do this without anger or sarcasm for it to work. Practice it several times before actually doing it in a real situation. Here are some practice examples:

– Stephie calls Mary a jerk. Mary says, "There may be some truth to that."

– Philip takes Sam's hat and is teasing him. Four of Philip's friends surround Sam. Sam says, "You must really like my hat. Either give it back when you're finished wearing it, or if you really love it, I'll give it to you as a gift. See you later."

– Joy tells Lori that she has ugly teeth. Lori says, "I wish I had teeth as beautiful as yours. Where did you get such pretty teeth?"

Now it is your turn. Practice agreeing when someone is trying to get you mad or into trouble.

• **Try to understand.** There may be some good reasons that you don't understand when someone tries to pick a fight. Maybe if you understood things better, you would be better able to say or do the right thing. When someone is coming at you and you aren't sure why, try saying something like, "I must have really done something to make you feel mad. What did I do? I sure would like you to tell me so that I won't make the same mistake again."

• **Apologize.** It takes a lot of guts to recognize when you have done something wrong and own up to the problem. Put yourself in someone else's shoes. Ask how you would feel if someone said or did the same thing to you that you just said or did to someone else. When you realize you did something wrong, be tough enough to go to that person and apologize. When said with meaning, the words, "I'm sorry" go a long way toward helping settle a problem so that no violence occurs. You can even apologize when you aren't sure that you did anything wrong but someone is really mad at you. At those times you might say something like, "I'm sorry if I did something that made you mad. I didn't mean to get you upset."

Put the Blame on Someone Else

Imagine that three guys see Bob walking home. They come over and show him cocaine, weed, or uppers. The pressure is on. They make him feel that to belong to their group or even feel safe he has to join them, but he really doesn't want to. Bob is quick on his feet and remembers that his Mom told him that he can always blame her when he doesn't want to join the group but is afraid of what might happen. He says, "Wow, I'd love to join you, but if I don't get home right away, my mom is gonna kill me!"

Another possibility is for Bob to say something like, "I'd love to (name the problem you want to avoid), but I'd (make an excuse) so (tell what you will do)." For instance:

- Steve is pressuring Jim to steal. Jim says, "Man, I'd love to own that stuff, but seeing how I'm always dropping things I'd just mess you up. Thanks for asking but I'd better stick to stuff I'm good at."
- Laticia, Josie, and Ellen ask Lisa to party with them. Lisa knows that alcohol is going to be there, and so are some guys who pressure girls to have sex. She isn't interested but doesn't want to look like a geek. She says, "I'd love to have a good time, but I gotta look after my little brother tonight or my Mom is gonna be real burned. Have a good time."

Who in your life can you blame so that you can avoid embarrassment in front of friends while making it clear that something terrible will happen to you if you join them?

Writing Letters or Keeping a Journal

When you are really angry, it is important that you find ways to let off steam. Many of the exercises we learned related to calming anger are intended to do just that. But it also can help to write down all of your thoughts and feelings in the form of a letter or in a journal. Most people choose to keep this information private, but there are times

when you might even share this writing with the people who made
you feel mad. You'll need to decide whether there is any benefit to
sharing these thoughts or whether it is just better to write them down
and keep them to yourself. Imagine that Raja teases Chen about his
clothes and hairstyle. Chen feels mad, and his first thought is to tease
him back. But he remembers that Raja and his friends are usually looking for trouble. He decides there is a good chance that if he gets into
it with Raja, the problem will only get worse. But he is steaming and
feels like belting Raja. He decides to write a note in his private journal: "I can't stand stupid Raja. What a jerk! I would really like to rip
his head off or just scream obscenities at him. But if I did, the jerk
would probably get his posse after me and I don't need that kind of
trouble. So I'm telling you, my friend, rather than him."

Decide to Let It Drop

It takes a lot of smarts and guts to walk away from a problem situation that could end up with someone getting hurt. Parents and teachers often tell kids to ignore when someone is trying to pick a fight or
hurt their feelings. Only you can decide whether getting hurt—or
hurting someone—is worth it. You also can decide to ignore the situation.

Every person's life is full of decisions to make. There are tons of
things that you can let bother you every day if you really want to. We
all need to learn how to let go of being bothered by things that really
aren't important. Deciding what is important to you is a major step
toward becoming mature.

Can you think of a bad situation that you are facing right now?
Picture yourself walking away from it. What happens? How would
your friends react? How do you think the other person or people you
are walking away from would react? How do you think your mother
or father would react if they knew you walked away? What do you
think about the idea that it takes a lot of self-confidence and guts to
walk away from trouble? What are some situations faced by people
your age that are hard to walk away from? Practice being in these situations with others. You might find that walking away often works best
when done after another strategy, such as "I-messages" or agreeing.
What do you think?

Taking Responsibility

At one high school in the Los Angeles area, teachers encourage students to take responsibility by letting them know that it is okay for them to tell on classmates who are breaking laws. At this school, students are actually given reward money for turning over the names of students who carry weapons, destroy school property, take things that belong to others, and deface school grounds with graffiti. The reward money is given when adults find that the student who was named actually did the misdeed.

In that school, care is taken to make sure that if one student tells on another, it is done in such a way that the student who broke the rules doesn't know who did the telling. That way, nobody has to worry about somebody wanting to get even. What do you think about that?

Not everyone agrees that giving away money is a good idea, but most think it is great when the school is safe for everyone. There just aren't enough hall monitors, principals, or teachers to make the school safe. As a student, the school belongs to you. In order for you to learn best, you have to feel safe. Together, students can make a huge difference in how things are at their school. It is important that you and your classmates find safe and effective ways to let all students know that dangerous or harmful behavior cannot be tolerated. Here are some questions to think about:

1. Are there things that make you feel unsafe at your school?

2. Are there things at your school that don't make you feel unsafe but you think make others feel unsafe?

3. Are there rules at your school that are supposed to protect you from the things that are happening in 1 and 2?

4. If you know that there are rules or laws that are supposed to keep others from doing these things, why do you think these things happen anyway?

5. What responsibilities do you think students should have for safety at the school?

6. What things do you think that you or others might do that can help send a message to the kids who do dangerous or hurtful stuff at school?

7. How do you think adults at your school would react if they received an unsigned note from someone like you telling about some-

thing dangerous that someone did or was about to do?

8. What do you think about the idea of rewarding students for telling on other students who are breaking laws and making the school less safe?

9. What plan do you think students should follow if they find out about possible dangers at school? Outside of school?

Who Will Miss Me If I Die?

Most kids think that nothing bad will ever happen to them. If you believe that, there is probably very little that will convince you otherwise. Stop and think about the fact that murder is one of the leading causes of death among teenagers. In fact, it is now the third leading cause of death among children ages 5 to 14. Only accidents not related to guns and cancer kill more kids. One U.S. child dies of a gunshot every two hours! And most kids who kill don't plan it that carefully. They get mad, get a weapon, and in the heat of their anger they blow someone away. Lots of times they get the gun before they even get mad because they think they need one to be cool.

Please realize that you can be a victim. Before you get even with someone who has been bugging you, think about what might happen if that person has a gun or knife. If they use it and you wind up hurt or dead, how would your mother, father, siblings, or other relatives feel? How would your friends feel? How would your coach feel? How do you think I [the teacher] would feel? How would others in this class feel? Can you picture a bunch of people you know in church with a minister talking about you while you are laying dead inside a casket? Are you ready to die? Or are there things you want to accomplish in life?

Think of someone you care about. What do you like about this person? What makes you want to be with him or her? Do you think that person knows how you feel? Do you think it is possible that your friend could die tomorrow? As unlikely as that is, if it did happen, how would you feel? What would you miss most about your friend? What do you think your friend would miss about you? If your friend was looking down at you from the "spirit world," what advice would you get? Have you ever known someone you cared about who died? Do you think they ever thought that they would die in the way they did? When they did?

Now think about some things you are doing that could get you killed. What might happen if you did the opposite of these things? Would you be willing to try some different ways for at least one week? What will you do?

From Always or Never to Mostly or Sometimes

Bad things happen to people. Some get sick, some of us have parents who get divorced, some have a parent who shows no interest, and some live in a dangerous neighborhood. What are some bad things that have happened to you? What bad things have happened to people you love?

We cannot control all of the bad or good things that happen to us. But one thing we can do when bad things happen is to stop using words like always or never. When we tell ourselves things like, "My mom *never* gives me what I want," "*Everybody* hates me," "My teacher is always unfair," "*Nobody* wants to play with me," "The *only* guys who anybody looks up to are the gang members," we lose control of making good decisions.

Think about it. If I begin to think, "My mom MOSTLY doesn't give me what I want," then that means that at least some times I get what I want. Can I learn to appreciate what I get rather than complain about what I don't? Can I look to mom for *some* things but not everything?

If I begin to think "Sometimes everybody hates me" or "Some people hate me most of the time," then I have a choice to hang around with the people who like me, stay away from the people who don't, and figure out ways to have more people like me more of the time.

Does that make sense to you? Many kids who think that bad things always happen to them and good things don't happen begin to expect that more bad things will keep happening. So they figure that they'd better protect themselves from these bad things. They get into fights more easily. They may buy guns or knives even when there is really little to fear. They may not try as hard as they should in school because they think it won't matter.

To practice this, complete the following sentences:

- The bad things that ALWAYS happen to me are. . . .
- The good things that NEVER happen to me are. . . .
- The people who are ALWAYS unfair are. . . .
- Everybody ALWAYS is mean when. . . .
- NOBODY ever is nice when. . . .

Now, change each sentence as follows:

- The bad things that SOMETIMES or MOSTLY happen to me are . . . .
- The good things that SOMETIMES or MOSTLY happen to me are. . . .
- The people who are SOMETIMES or MOSTLY unfair are. . . .
- A person who is MOSTLY unfair to me that was at least one time fair was. . . . Tell what they did when they were fair.
- SOME people are mean when. . . .
- SOMETIMES people are nice when. . . .

Learn to Mediate

Many students are learning how to help others and themselves talk out problems rather than do something more dangerous. There are specific steps people follow when negotiating differences. A person who works with other people to help them solve their problems is a mediator. Anyone who believes that nonviolent solutions can be reached through discussing, compromising, and agreeing can become a mediator. If the Arabs and Israelis can mind mediated solutions to some of their problems, don't you think two gangs can agree to solve their problems nonviolently?

If the school has a mediation program, consider joining it. Schools in all different kinds of neighborhoods have started programs because kids need to know that there are other ways to solve problems rather than get violent.

If your school doesn't have a program, then maybe you can talk to the principal, teacher, or counselor and see if they can help get one at school.

In mediation, two kids with a beef with each other agree to meet with someone who can help them figure out a solution to the problem. The mediator is someone who isn't a friend of either of the students who are arguing. It is a person who is neutral. The mediator knows how to help kids talk with each other so that they can figure out solutions to problems they have together. When you meet with a mediator, it is nobody else's business. Things you say are private. Usually the mediator asks each kid to say the following things to each other:

- Tell the other person what he or she did that is bugging you. Both kids take turns telling each other.
- Make sure that each person has correctly heard the other by asking each to tell the other what he or she heard.
- Tell the other person what he or she does that you like. Think of at least two things that you like or respect about the other person. Each student takes a turn.
- Tell the other person what you want him or her to do differently that you think will solve the problem for you. You need to think of at least two solutions. Once again, each person takes a turn.
- Talk with each other until both people can figure out how they can solve the problem. Both people keep talking until they figure out at least one solution that both can live with.
- Both sides shake hands. Each writes down the solution and signs it.

Having Hope

Think about someone you don't know but look up to. Maybe this is a sports star, musician, or doctor. How do you think that person got to be so successful? Do you think it was just luck or do you think that person worked hard? How can you find out? Many successful people like to hear from kids who would like to turn out the way they did. Why not write a letter and ask that person questions that you would like to know? How about taking a risk and asking someone you admire? Maybe you'd rather go to the library and read an autobiography about someone you look up to.

How would you like people to remember you? Suppose that you could be anyone you want so that you could be remembered and respected as you would like. How would you live your life? What is most important for people to remember? What are some things you can do right now as a student that might make it possible for things to turn out the way you want some day? It may sound silly, and you've heard it before, but "Today is the first day of the rest of your life." What can you do today to get where you want to be?

Mental Weight Lifting

Lots of students want to get strong. They go to the gym and work out. Some lift weights, others do exercise, some run. Most kids don't know that, just as you can work out to become physically strong, it is possible to work out mentally by doing the right exercises. In fact, most champions do both! They get their bodies ready for competition while at the same time practicing mental exercises. They learn to picture themselves doing an activity before they are actually doing it.

In many ways, we are who we think we are. For example, a basketball player will actually picture himself making free throws. He will see himself at the line, ball in hand, with other players around watching. He actually feels himself release the ball. Swish! Olympic champion Jackie Joyner-Kersee visualizes her race before she runs.

If you want positive things to happen, you must first learn to make positive pictures in your mind. You must see yourself doing what you want. You must see yourself achieving your goal or dream.

You must first see and hear yourself walking away from a possible fight before you actually do it. You must be able to hear yourself saying nonviolent words or statements before you will actually use them. You can practice doing this. You become mentally tough by repeating the following sentences to yourself. Make a habit of saying each of these several times every day and then see what happens. Eventually, you will just choose to say the ones that work best for you:

- I can handle this.
- I'm prepared.
- If someone bugs me, I won't take it personally.
- This could get rough, but I will know what to say.
- Just stay calm and count.
- Just stay calm and breathe.
- My heart is pumping! Time to calm down!

- I need to just think about what I have to do.
- I am smart.
- I am able.
- I care about people and they care about me.

"Dear Uncle Smarty"

Some of you may be familiar with advice given to grown-ups in a column called Dear Abby. People write to Abby with their problems, and Abby gives them the best advice she can. Not everyone always agrees with her answers, but the basic idea makes sense.

Either alone, with a partner, or in a group, read through the following letters written to "Uncle Smarty." Answer them the best way you can with nonviolent solutions you've learned regarding calming anger and problem solving.

Dear Uncle Smarty,

a. My brother is retarded and rides the school bus with me and my friends. Some big jerks call him names, and I get mad. Those guys are bigger than I am and, anyhow, I just don't want to get beat up. What should I do?

b. Phyllis, Julia, and Samantha are always picking on me. They call me names and make faces. I get so mad but I don't know what to do. I don't really want to, but I think I'm going to have to fight Phyllis because she's the leader and I have to show that I'm tough. Is that my best solution?

c. These guys at my school are really gross. They call me and some of the other girls names like "slut." Even worse, they occasionally grab my breasts. Teachers are never around when this happens so I don't think anyone is going to do anything. I can't stand it anymore. What should I do?

d. There's a new kid at school who acts really bossy. Even though he gets into a lot of trouble and doesn't follow the rules, it's like everyone thinks he's cool. Even some of my friends are starting to hang around him. I think he's into drugs and he makes like he was in a gang where he used to live. I don't want to hang around him but my friends do, and unless I hang around him, I'm not going to see much of my friends. I just don't know what to do.

Using What You Learn

List five recent situations where either you or someone you know was tempted to get into a fight. This could be either physical (with fists) or verbal (through name calling, for example). Next to each situation, write down the strategies you are learning from our lessons on Calming Anger or Problem Solving that you think could help in each situation if it happened again.

End Note to Teacher: After you have taught and shared these activities, you can reinforce learning by using the last closure activity on a regular or occasional basis. Encourage students to share solutions with each other, including new ones or variations they think might work better. You may begin discussion by asking for incidents experienced by your students or by using a current school, community, or world event of violence. Students can be instructed to apply their learning to these situations. In actuality, the activities are a means to identify concerns and focus on solutions. There will be no real end to curricula on violence prevention until the day when there is no longer any violence.

Creating Safe Schools: 25 Options for Increasing Safety

Educating children so their values, attitudes, and social skills become less aggressive and hostile is as important as instructing them in reading, math, and science. As we said earlier, teaching responsibility always has been an unacknowledged important "R" in schools, but now it is more important than ever.

The behavioral changes educators seek are incremental, though, and they take longer to achieve than most of us would like. It will take time to see results filter into society, and it also will take time to see the changes affect schools. In the meantime, we must adopt other measures to reduce violent episodes and, just as important, lessen the perception that school is a violent place. This chapter describes 25 ways to improve school safety while we patiently await more long-lasting transformations in students and society.

Some of the measures are short-term; others should be an ongoing part of the daily routine. Some of the suggestions will seem modest, and others will appear too harsh. This reflects the reality that all schools are different. In some districts, no student has ever come to school with a concealed gun. In others, this is a daily or weekly event. Faculties must choose and adapt the suggestions that are appropriate for their individual schools. In addition, they may want to generate other suggestions that address local situations.

An important general tool in the antiviolence crusade is the creation of a perception of safety so all students understand that the adults in charge are both concerned about them and prepared to take actions to make the school a place where they can learn without fear. When students believe that violence is a natural certainty, they, like adults, fear it—but they also accept it.

The fear leads to an increase in weapons and other defensive actions; some students decide that a gang provides safety (if only from fellow gang members). The acceptance of violence leads to the belief that it is okay to be violent and that it is better to strike first—and fast. The more we establish a perception of safety, the more we can change violence that breeds upon itself.

The key leader in this effort is the building principal. More than any other individual, the principal sets the tone for the entire school. However, the principal cannot go it alone; everyone must be involved. No one can do everything, but everyone can do something. Faculty, students, and community members must create a partnership to make school a safe place.

1. Establish High Visibility of Adults

By far, the most effective, inexpensive means of promoting school safety is to station adults throughout the building. In schools with a history of violence, adults with walkie-talkies should walk the hallways in pairs in a manner similar to community watch programs. In other schools, the mere presence of adults without walkie-talkies can be a moderating influence.

Administrators or teachers on administrative assignment can be very helpful in this effort. Parent volunteers who come to school on a regular basis often provide a moderating influence on student behavior. All staff members and parents can use time in the hallways to establish positive relationships with students in an informal way. Those relationships can be very useful in keeping on top of possible trouble before it begins. Caring adults who take an active interest at school convey messages of nurturance and safety.

2. Involve Students in the Visibility Effort

Many students are willing to become involved in "neighborhood watch" efforts within their school. Like adults, students can keep an eye on behaviors that occur within the school, and they also can be trained to report inappropriate behaviors to adults. At no time should they be permitted to confront violent behavior. They are simply observers involved in making school a safer place.

Some schools have been successful in reaching out to "at-risk" students by inviting them to join such an effort. In a few schools, students are the main players in these efforts. Remember, though, that you must closely define the parameters of appropriate "monitoring" behavior.

Reseda High School's WARN program in Reseda, California, encourages students to anonymously report dangerous behavior either directly to school authorities or to an 800 number that is open 24 hours a day. This program was started in one of the "safer" high schools of Los Angeles after a student was killed on school grounds. Apparently, several students knew that the shooter was armed before the incident but failed to report it to authorities. Too often, concerned students do not tell anyone about danger because they don't have a safe, easy way to do it.

We can envision programs like Reseda's becoming affiliated with neighborhood or community Crime Stoppers programs. If necessary, rewards can be offered for reliable information about the presence of weapons in a manner similar to Crime Stoppers. In fact, there is a Scholastic Crime Stoppers Program, which was started in 1983 by Officer Larry Weida. It proved successful in Fairview High School in Boulder, Colorado, and since then Officer Wieda has had more than 800 requests for information from educational institutions.[1]

3. Meet with Gang Leaders

A considerable amount of school violence is related to gang growth. Sometimes it is effective to meet with gang leaders, inviting

---

[1] For more information about the Scholastic Crime Stoppers Program, contact Det. Larry Wieda, 1805 33rd St., Boulder, CO 80301. Phone: (303) 441-3327. Fax: (303)441-4327. More information about the Crime Stoppers Program is available on the World Wide Web at http://www.c-s-i.org/.

them to suggest solutions to make the school a "neutral zone" for gangs.

Lessons Learned

"I was walking down the street and I seen this fat guy who owe me money and he did not pay me yet, so I walked up to him and kick him in the chest, punch him in the eye kick him below the belt and elbowed him in the back then he fell and I started kicking him in the head, face, stomach basic all over his body then I look through his wallet and took my 25 cents. I wouldn't do it again because I felt bad because he was bleeding and cry over 25 cents I wouldn't of did it if he paid me my money I'm 18 now and I might go to jail so that would stop me from doing it in the future."

— A male student

It is important that gang leaders are dealt with in a respectful, firm manner, but gangs should not be permitted to "represent" a school with colors, hats, clothing, or symbols. Beepers and headphones should not be permitted. Gang-related graffiti should be destroyed. All of these rules can and should be established by school authorities, but gang leaders can be "consulted" or involved in deciding the best ways to ensure that the rules will be followed. In communities where gangs are prevalent, their participation and suggestions are often the difference between successful or failed antiviolence programs. When gang members are encouraged to redirect their sense of leadership, they often will see to it that the rules are enforced.

4. Develop Community Service Programs for Students

Empathy and altruism are effective antidotes to violence (Curwin 1992, Mendler 1992). Too many youngsters who react violently to a situation lack empathy. They just don't care. Before young people get to this point—and even after they have crossed over—it is absolutely essential to reawaken them to caring for others.

A body of research demonstrates that empathy may be inherited (Zahn-Wexler and Radke-Yarrow 1982). Infants as young as one or two days old show signs of empathy in that they cry sympathetically in response to the cries of other infants in a manner not elicited by other equally loud, provocative stimuli. We believe that some students lose this capacity for sympathy because of the personal hurts and wounds that they have experienced from others who are supposed to love and care. Empathy is reawakened by involving and empowering children in activities where they are in positions to give and reach out to others.

Programs where students adopt a grandparent, adopt a pet, assist a physically disabled person, or tutor younger students can be very effective at reteaching violence-prone children to care. Retirees can be especially helpful in this effort. We know of instances at Oatka Residential Center in Rush, New York, in which juvenile criminals were required to work with elderly people, often with impressive results. It is touching to watch a "hardened" street child comb a patient's hair and read her books. Many elderly folks who are searching for meaning in their later years love volunteering to help students socially and academically. Forward-thinking professionals and citizens at Hope Meadows in Champagne County, Illinois, converted an abandoned army base into a community of single-family foster homes. The recipe is foster parents, foster children, senior citizens, and mental health services creating a network of love, support, discipline, and intervention. The seniors move into low-cost apartments in this converted community and provide loving, nurturing support to the children at school and in the community. Lives are being turned around among children with horrific social histories. If this kind of change can be done at a community level, a smaller version can certainly be done at school. Getting students involved in mentoring programs or neighborhood watch efforts described in the first suggestion are often win-win situations.

5. Report and Prosecute All Criminal Aggression and Violence

The police need to be notified when behaviors occur on school grounds that would be considered violations of the law anyplace else. Although police and the courts often are overwhelmed, aggressors need to understand the consequences of their behaviors, and other students need to know that their safety is protected. If nothing else, notifying police about an incident sends a signal to the entire student body that aggressive or violent behavior will not be tolerated.

In many instances, school fights are dealt with too leniently. We certainly do not advocate making each and every instance of violence a police matter. For example, a pushing match is best dealt with through conflict mediation rather than an arrest. But when a serious assault occurs, police notification along with a suspension signals that assault on school grounds is just as inappropriate and illegal as it is anywhere else.

Each time a serious law is broken, charges should be pressed. Faculty members need to define the phrase "serious law" so the issue of whether to press charges is not disputed at the time of an incident. Obvious infractions such as bringing a gun to school are easy. But what about a pocket knife or a box cutter? Why do you charge a student: for concealed possession of a weapon, displaying it, or using it? Your local police can help you establish some very simple guidelines that are appropriate for your school's circumstances.

6. Handle Minor Discipline Problems with Effective Consequences

Rule breaking and disorderly conduct should not be permitted in school. We have become far too tolerant of "minor" rule violations, which has slowly but certainly contributed to an atmosphere of anything goes.

Society does not self-destruct in giant steps. Each time we accept a rule violation, we slip further down the slippery slope of the wrong kind of tolerance. Some children will always go beyond the limits we set. The more we expand those limits, the further students push them and the more anxious everyone becomes. All rule violations should be addressed, no matter how small.

If a rule exists in school, all staff members must enforce it regardless of individual views. Too often, staff members look the other way, especially when they find a rule disagreeable. That sends the wrong signal to students: The only rules you really have to follow are those that you find agreeable.

When developing consequences, consistency is more important than severity. For that reason, we advocate being fair without treating everyone the same. Having a range of consequences allows educators to enforce a rule each time it is broken by being as tough as necessary. Students know there is predictability in that rules are enforced, and educators maintain the flexibility to deal with situations in a caring, individualized manner.

Infrequent but severe consequences are usually counterproductive in changing behavior. The main role of a consequence is to teach that some behaviors are unacceptable. When consequences are made too severe, they lose their usefulness. Deterrents usually work best with those who rarely break rules. We also must be careful about the glamour effect of harsh consequences. Students who want to prove themselves as "tough" often engage in behaviors that have harsh consequences to prove their courage.

Great care must be taken to ensure that rules truly reflect the values of the school and that they reflect current realities. Many rules exist simply because they have been handed down year after year after year. All rules must be tested against the school's current values and be relevant to existing social realities. Discard all rules that are enforced haphazardly, or modify them to be more realistic.

In many schools, staff members continue to argue about the relative value of having rules involving food, hats, and personal stereos. In our view, the best rules are those that support learning. Having rules that offend the taste of some faculty members and really do not support learning serves little purpose. In some schools, students wear hats in class with no negative consequences. If, on the other hand, hats show affiliation with a gang or have some other meaning that gets in the way of learning, they should be barred.

Having a safe school environment supports learning. Unfortunately, when small acts of disorder are tolerated, more and worse behavior will follow. As Jackson Toby points out (1994), a school that lets students wander the halls when they're supposed to be in class or a school that fails to clean up trash and graffiti invites students to further test the limits of unacceptable behavior.

With rare exception, violators should be expected to clean or repair the damage they do. If it's unknown who did something, the responsibility for cleaning and repairing should be shared by all students who are part of the learning community. If someone steals, then the violator should not only make restitution but be required to give a personal object or service to the individual who was harmed. Again, if the violator is unknown, the group should be involved in finding ways to make proper restitution to the individual.

Students should be kindly but clearly reminded to pick up their mess in the cafeteria and hallways. Stu Agor, principal of Irondequoit High School near Rochester, New York, was dismayed at the poor condition in which his students left their cafeteria. One day on the loud speaker, he appealed to their sense of school pride and good manners, asking them to throw out not only their own garbage but other discarded food and refuse if they saw it. By the end of that day, the cafeteria was in much better condition and only periodic reminders were needed to maintain the improvement. Too often we tolerate, ignore, and then erupt. Maybe all it really takes is to consistently ask students to respectfully do the right things more of the time.

Remember that you don't need all students on board. You do need to establish a climate that supports responsible behavior. We have found that schools that adopt these kinds of practices, preferably in collaboration with parents, have better overall discipline and less serious problems. When parents don't collaborate in creating rules, it is best to garner their support by explaining the rules to them before there are any problems.

7. Treat Weapon Possession Seriously

All students with weapons must be treated seriously. Long-term suspensions, reports to the police, and in certain instances permanent removal should be the norm rather than the exception. In the absence of an alternative program, students can receive instruction off-site (e.g., home tutoring). The most important signal to send is that you can remain on school grounds when your behavior is congruent with the basic safety requirements of a civilized community. Weapons are not a part of such a community.

Lessons Learned

"What I think people should do if they are in a fight is to talk about it like we did. At first you will feel scared about but if you don't talk about it will get worse."

— A female student

8. Nurture a Violence-Free Atmosphere

Although increasing numbers of adults and students fear violence at school, the fact is that schools in virtually all communities are probably the safest place for children. This is especially true for students living in gang-dominated, drug-infested, inner-city neighborhoods. We need to keep schools safe by reinforcing and adopting practices that clearly and certainly promote safety.

Although it may sound "hokey," developing antiviolence placards, sayings, and artwork that are prominently displayed throughout the school can set or reinforce a desirable tone. Along with specific actions to curb violence, we also must deal at every level with the psychology of hope. Positive signs, drawings, and sayings can meaningfully contribute to the development of prosocial attitudes, thoughts, and behaviors.

To promote their new peer mediation program at Foller High School, students placed signs and illustrated placards around the building with messages like KEEP YOUR POWER . . . TALK IT OUT and THE CHOICE IS YOURS: STAY COOL. Jefferson Middle School in Rochester, New York, has bulletin boards in the halls with reminders of positive phrases to use when stressed (e.g., "When you finish that, could you . . . ," "Thanks anyhow, but not now.").

9. Open the School to Adult Learners

We believe that the presence of adult learners can have a calming effect on the entire school climate. Although it is financially understandable, it makes little educational sense to relegate dropouts over the age of 21 to night school. Older students who have "been there" can provide younger students with a perspective others can't. Further, adults who return to school often are more serious about their studies because they have already experienced the very limited employment options available to those with little formal education.

We have heard encouraging preliminary reports from a few urban high schools in Chicago that are blending their teenage with adult learners in that they support the view of calmer, more academically focused classes. While the jury is still out on effectiveness, young people need to see and experience their elders struggling to succeed at school because they realize they have limited options without an education. Opening the school doors in meaningful, inviting ways to all law-abiding segments of the community makes it much more likely that the kind of networking we advocate will occur. We applaud another somewhat less risky and inexpensive initiative of some of the tougher Philadelphia schools, which are creating parent lounges in their buildings complete with free coffee. We need to send a clear message: Our school wants you there!

10. Conduct Regular, Unannounced Weapons and Drug Searches

When weapons and drugs are a serious concern, announce to all—including parents—that regular, unannounced searches within acceptable legal parameters are part of the school routine. Depending upon the circumstances, it would be wise to seek police assistance to ensure that federal, state, and local statutes are observed during such probes.

11. Use Rehabilitated Prisoners as Tutors or Big Brothers

This is a win-win situation. It provides former prisoners with an opportunity to contribute meaningfully by serving as mentors to students at risk. Such adults often gain quick credibility and "respect" because they can identify with the children and can speak from both the head and the heart. Students gain the advantage of becoming involved with someone who has made positive changes in life and can offer advice and insight.

The police can help by providing names of appropriate individuals or government agencies that can provide names and addresses. Half-way houses and drug rehabilitation agencies are additional resources that might be interested in collaborating with the school.

12. Use Lights

Conventional wisdom suggests that good lighting discourages unwanted entry. Citizens are normally advised to leave on lights when they are vacationing to discourage burglars. A high school principal recently told us, however, that local police advised him to either brighten the school at night or leave it completely dark. Apparently, potential vandals may be as reluctant to enter a completely dark building as they are one that is well lighted. Given the potential savings in power bills, we are intrigued by this second alternative. Before choosing to leave the school dark, conduct a security analysis. Your local police or security consultant can provide assistance with this decision.

13. Install Video or Closed-Circuit Systems

It is sad but true that money that could be better used elsewhere is spent on video systems as a deterrent to violence. Some school districts have found the need to install video cameras in strategic locations throughout the building. Many of them have found that when video cameras are used, behavior improves—at least for the short-term—in hard to monitor places such as buses and hallways.

Even better is when schools use videos to work with students to improve behavior. Some challenging students aren't aware of how their behavior looks. They are often lectured about what they do, but too often they simply do not have a picture of how they look when they are engaging in objectionable behavior. We have seen some students with a look of complete surprise when they are observing themselves on a video. Contrasting the behavior they are seeing with more appropriate behavior is the goal. Using videos that show such contrasting behavior can be helpful in teaching acceptable behavior.

14. Mix Faculty and Student Parking at High Schools

This creates an adult presence in the parking lot, which can serve as a deterrent to trouble making. Faculty concerned about car vandalism might consider that this arrangement may make the singling out of a specific faculty member more difficult. It seems logical that if somebody wants to deface the car of a faculty member, finding the car in the "faculty only" parking would be much easier than finding that same car in the larger general parking lot.

15. Establish Safe Homes on the Route to School

It is very important that the entire community become involved in combating the problem of community and school violence. Though school is usually the safest, least violent place within a community, students often are afraid traveling to and from the building. Some communities have successfully established "safe" homes for children in which they can seek refuge when they feel endangered. Citizens on the route to school may volunteer to make their homes such a refuge by signing on with the school and then signaling students that their home is a safe haven by keeping a light burning on the porch or a sign posted in the door or window.

16. Trim Shrubbery to Limit Hiding Places for Weapons or People

Many schools have found that metal detectors are essentially ineffective in eliminating weapons because of easy access through windows and unguarded doors. To this end, it is useful to trim shrubbery around all windows and doors so it is more difficult to sneak people, weapons, or anything else into school.

17. Consider Hiring a Police Officer

Until recently, the thought of having a regular police officer on duty at school was mortifying to all but those in the most crime-infested neighborhoods and schools. However, with the increased perception of danger in many schools, hiring a police officer as a regular staff member makes sense.

The presence of police authority can itself be a deterrent to would-be criminal conduct. But in addition, most police officers have received considerable training in crisis prevention and resolution. Today's police officer is often well-prepared with an impressive array of interpersonal skills that can become an important problem-solving resource in the school. Other benefits are the officer's authority to make an arrest or to simply set up connections between school and the criminal justice system.

Arrangements for an officer often need to include city and police officials. Some school police officers are paid with municipal funds; others are funded with school dollars. The schools of Raleigh and Greenville, North Carolina, appear to be effectively integrating police officers in the overall educational process.

18. Simulate Real-Life Consequences of Violence

Threats and scare tactics have a temporary effect. But we believe it is important to create partnerships with hospitals, prisons, and police so that students can experience the grim realities of violence.

It's true that exposure to harsh consequences is rarely sufficient in changing behavior. And any intervention needs to be done with thought and care as part of a larger effort to teach positive values. But students who are physically aggressive or who bring weapons to school would benefit from spending a Saturday night in the emergency room so they experience the pain and misery caused by violence.

Some programs like "Scared Straight" use violent, incarcerated criminals to educate children in the consequences of violence with no-nonsense language and an in-your-face attitude. While these programs are rarely effective for longer than the weeks or months when they are used as a sole intervention, we believe that they can serve as a wake-up call when paired with more therapeutic interventions. We need to remind judges about the importance of a consequence like a night in jail after a youngster's first serious offense so there is a better chance that a lasting impression will be left during the formative years. Although the most hardened youngsters are unlikely to benefit and may even view the consequence as a badge of courage, we believe that many more youth would benefit from the taste of misery when it is coupled with educational/psychological follow-up such as action plans and restitution.

Lessons Learned

"I pranked the 9-1-1 emergency telephone. I was with two girls and also my best friend. I did it because I was "dared" to do it and plus I knew that I would get a good laugh out of it. And I kinda felt good about it, because my friends did laugh about it. The only thing that probably could have stopped me from doing it would be, if I could have seen the future consequences of this Act."

— A male student

---

19. Create a School Violence Action Plan

Violence is a terrifying experience for all, and it is even worse when we are not psychologically prepared for it. Preparing psychologically is important because adults in charge must maintain a calm, in-charge attitude when a crisis occurs. Although such incidents are still rare, if a student pulls out a gun in class or takes classmates hostage, administrators and staff members must be as prepared as possible to deal with the incident. Perhaps a more frequently occurring problem requiring a school action plan is fighting. All staff should be trained in knowing what to do and what not to do if they are confronted with student fighting.

The specifics of a school's action plan need to take into account the physical plant as well as people. It is impossible to create one plan for all schools. However, certain common issues and actions can be anticipated.

- Develop ways to immediately signal staff members that a crisis is occurring; it's a good idea to develop both open signals and coded signals. All staff should be informed of specific cues that warrant a safety crisis. In general, when the cues are present, it is best to lock doors, secure rooms, and take immediate shelter. Again, it is best for each school to consider its circumstances and resources, and consult with safety experts or law enforcement professionals in developing these procedures. Be careful to not lock out others who may be in a vulnerable area, like hallways, and are seeking shelter. If at all possible, information should be given through the school's communication system along with specific instructions.

- Decide where the command post will be. The office usually serves this purpose, since communication systems are centralized there. If the location selected as the command post is itself the site of the crisis, a back-up site should be identified along with methods of communication to inform staff and students.

- Teach everyone to shelter themselves in place in the unlikely event of gunfire. In general, it is best to use basic duck-and-cover techniques such as getting on the floor and covering the head or getting under desks and tables, lying face down. In a classroom, it is best to stay away from windows, doors, and outer walls. Although it is necessary to get into immediate positions of safety, be ready to move quickly.

- Contact law enforcement and health authorities. The plan needs to identify who gets called (i.e., police, fire department, paramedics, ambulances). Usually dialing 911 is sufficient.

- Decide who will manage the information flow to parents, community, and press.

- After the crisis ends, it is necessary to process the incident. First, everyone needs to be checked for injuries and someone needs to account for all students. It is important that educators stay with children until they are picked up by a parent or guardian. In particular, any children who were directly involved in the incident or who were eyewitnesses may need to share information with investigators. Accompanying them while they do so or ensuring parental presence is important. These students should also see a mental health professional following the incident for assessment and possible intervention. Any other students who feel affected by the incident should have help available upon request. At the very least, a collaborative effort between school and outside mental health professionals along with educators is needed. It is best to have these pieces in place before a crisis. While the specific components of a crisis plan may vary based on needs and resources, an approach to crisis management like the Dallas Independent School District's Crisis Management Plan provides a comprehensive set of guidelines and actions.

20. Require Each Classroom to Have a Violence Action Plan

Just as a school violence action plan is necessary, so is one for each classroom. The classroom violence action plan is likely to be more frequently used because minor incidents of violence occur more often. To minimize the negative impact of violent student behavior, the teacher and students must know what to do when such behavior occurs. For example, students need to know that if objects are thrown, the students are to duck while the teacher deals with the problem student. Identify a student who will go to the office for help. This kind of structure and knowledge often reduces the anxiety many students feel when around an aggressive classmate. Teachers should assure students that these behaviors will occur rarely, if ever, because the students are developing the skills to express themselves appropriately. These contingency plans are to make sure we all know what to do when someone strikes out in violent ways. If someone is being intimidated, bullied, or picked on, a classroom plan defines specific strategies for students and the teacher.

21. Establish a Dress Code

More and more students use violence to ensure that they get the material things to which they feel entitled. With so much attention on acquiring clothes and possessions as a sign of prestige and power, those whose lives are immersed in poverty are especially vulnerable. But with a dress code in place, students can concentrate on academic issues instead of who has the flashiest gold chain or the most fashionable clothes. With a dress code, clothing becomes a nonissue.

All students need are a pair of the right colored pants or skirt (usually black), plain shirt, and possibly a tie. Some secondary schools in Chattanooga, Tennessee, have been using dress codes for a while and feel good about reductions in undesirable behavior. Paradoxically, dress codes free students to appreciate and take pride in the real, sustaining elements of their culture without continually being concerned about looking acceptable by current peer standards.

School uniforms are a more radical variation of dress codes. At one time, uniforms were the domain of parochial education. People once thought they stifled individuality, but opinions have changed. Uniforms, like dress codes, equalize class, race, and other variables that set the stage for hostility. Uniforms can have positive effects on violence reduction, as seen in Figure 5.1.

We worked in an upper middle-class Jewish day school outside of Los Angeles that takes as many as one-third of its students for free or reduced rates. Because of required uniforms, no one knows who is on scholarship, and students can participate in social experiences that might otherwise be out of their reach. We endorse the use of mandatory uniforms in schools that believe they can be useful.

22. Have Parents Ride School Buses

Many teachers report that it is in locations outside the classroom, such as school buses, that problems begin and end. This is not surprising in that these are less supervised places. After all, it can be extremely taxing for a bus driver to drive safely and supervise children. (Though it is possible to do, as evidenced by the many fine school bus drivers in Rochester, New York, who have been trained in applicable methods from the *Discipline with Dignity* program.)

The bus is one place in which increased supervision can be beneficial, and involving parents is an effective way to ensure a safer ride.

Figure 5.1

**EFFECTS OF UNIFORMS IN THE LONG BEACH, CALIF.,
UNIFIED SCHOOL DISTRICT**

Type of Incident / Number of Incidents

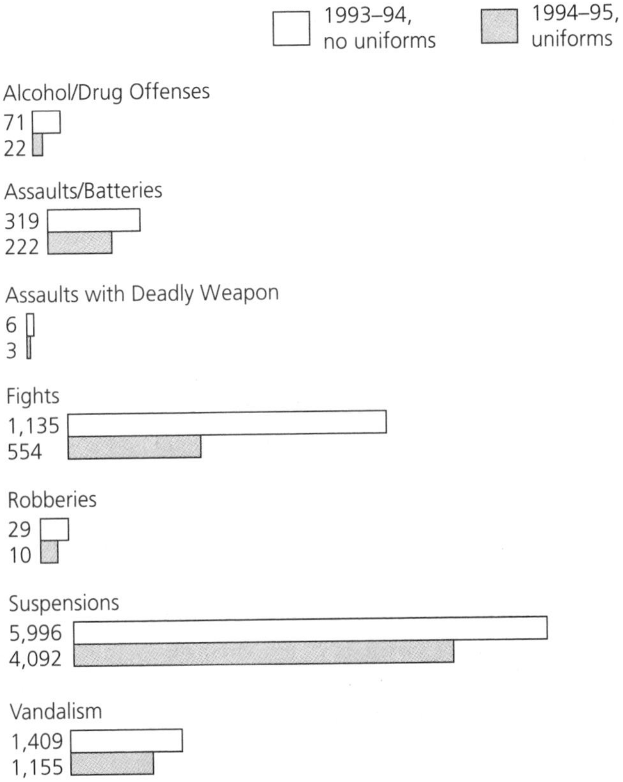

☐ 1993–94, no uniforms   ▧ 1994–95, uniforms

Alcohol/Drug Offenses
71
22

Assaults/Batteries
319
222

Assaults with Deadly Weapon
6
3

Fights
1,135
554

Robberies
29
10

Suspensions
5,996
4,092

Vandalism
1,409
1,155

Source: Long Beach, Calif., Unified School District.

For example, parents could be required to ride the bus with a child for a prescribed time period. Adults from the community could volunteer on a rotating basis to supervise behavior on the bus. Pairs of adults who are empowered by the school to supervise behavior can be an effective, visible presence on a bus. We would like to see older student "buddies" assigned to challenging younger children for friendship and mentoring on the bus. In extreme cases, video equipment can be used.

Even better is to instruct students in appropriate conduct at the start of the school year. Some school districts have successfully enforced standards of basic decency and respect by staging instances of respectful and disrespectful behavior and then showing videotapes to student bus riders while teaching about proper and improper behavior. One school we know of took videos of its two worst-behaved busloads of students. The goal was to show students the difference between their actions and what was appropriate behavior. The findings were eye-opening both to students and staff. The most problematic students were often the least aware of how they acted. The video turned out to be a very effective means by which to provide instructional feedback on the consequences of behavior. Incidents of misbehavior dramatically dropped on the buses.

23. Require that Parents Accompany Their Children to School

In extreme cases of disruptive behavior where a student may have to be expelled, it can be effective to offer parents and guardians the option of attending school with a child for a predetermined interval. It is not usually necessary or wise for the parent to sit in on each class. The parent can be in the building on call, can escort the student from class to class, or can speak to the student two or three times each day.

If a student literally needs a parent every moment of the day to assert authority, then he or she is in the wrong program and needs to receive schooling in a different environment. Usually, one week is all that's needed to gauge the effectiveness of this alternative. In less extreme cases, this practice can also be an effective way of getting parents and their children focused on what needs to get done in order to be successful in school. Or, if necessary, they can be directed to other school, counseling, or community resources that might help the situation.

24. Involve Students as Decision Makers and Problem Solvers

In our discipline work, we often find that including students in decisions about classroom rules, principles, and routines dramatically increases their commitment to them. Most schools make far too little effort to empower the most precious, abundant resource we have:

children. After all, students often are as concerned about violence as their teachers and other adults. They have a large stake in both problem identification and solution. We should not protect children from the realities they will face outside of school. School should be practice for the real world.

All committees dealing with issues of violence should include students. All proposed solutions should be shared with students before they become policy. After all, it's their school. Educators are there to facilitate and promote students' education, but students are the primary consumers in the school. As such, they should have a say in developing procedures and policies that affect them.

25. Encourage Students to Sign Pledge Cards

In some schools, students sign pledge cards against violence, similar to initiatives by Students Against Drunk Driving and Mothers Against Drunk Driving. Figure 5.2 shows a sample pledge card created at Tarboro High School in Tarboro, North Carolina. After students read and sign the pledge card, they can receive discounts on goods and services from participating local businesses when they present their card. Violations of the pledge card lead to loss of use for a prescribed time or until restitution is made.

Figure 5.2
THE S.A.V.E. PLEDGE
(STUDENTS AGAINST VIOLENCE EVERYWHERE)

I pledge to help end violence everywhere. I pledge to ask for help if I am ever faced with a situation that could result in violence. I pledge not to be violent at home, at school, or in the community. I also pledge that if I see any type of violence I will report it and/or try to help the people that are involved.

I have read the pledge and I understand it. If I violate this pledge I will face the consequences of school, local, and state laws.

Thank you for your commitment to end violence everywhere.

The S.A.V.E. Committee

Student Signature_____ Date_____

Conclusion

The theme is as old as the United States, and in some ways it defines the nation's spirit. A bully runs roughshod over weak victims who are afraid to fight back. Then a single hero emerges who appears to be no match for the bigger, stronger tormentor. But because the hero is courageous and is on the side of right, he vanquishes the oppressor. We could be talking about a John Wayne or Clint Eastwood western; a blue-collar worker turned boxing champ named Rocky; or a group of inner-city kids and their visionary teacher who defy the naysayers, master Advanced Placement Calculus, and inspire a movie called *Stand and Deliver.*

In the United States, we have always culturally defined ourselves as champions of the underdog who overcomes great odds to win in the name of righteousness. Now we are faced with a new bully that terrorizes and generates fear wherever it goes. This bully is *violence*, and it is time for people of courage and virtue to take a stand. Simply fortifying our homes, schools, and workplaces with fences, barriers, and metal detectors is not going to make us safer—nor will it increase our financial, emotional, or cultural prosperity. Antiviolence measures such as gun sweeps, searches without probable cause, and easy access wiretaps carry great costs. It is unacceptable and unfortunate that our values of freedom and liberty are threatened by a cultural shift to acquiring safety at all costs.

In 1995, California Governor Pete Wilson suggested public spankings of youthful graffiti taggers. Throughout the United States, violent children increasingly are prosecuted as adults with a "lock 'em up and throw away the key" mentality. Simplistic solutions like these may sound good to angry, frustrated voters, but they are futile, desperate measures that in reality will contribute to increased violence by youth. There is no quick fix.

The trend to fortify against violence rather than confront it directly challenges our hero image of ourselves and our cultural value of standing up to a bully. Short-term fortifications might be prudent, but the long-term answer requires three basic elements: teaching nonviolent values, modeling nonviolent behavior, and teaching alternative behaviors to violence.

This book defines our vision of how schools can change the future. We believe that schools have a critical role in teaching antiviolence values. We need not look forward to lives based in fear, retribution, fortification, and loss of the international dream shared by parents of children everywhere. Instead, we can create a future where people get along with each other, cooperate, behave altruistically, and don't kill one another. We know full well that a generation of parents appears lost, that children have dangerous attitudes and are prone to violent solutions to aggression and hostility, and that the proliferation of weapons available to students is obscene. But the students of today are the parents of tomorrow. When education is correctly defined and delivered today, we create a more positive tomorrow with better jobs, lives, and societies.

We are well aware that there is an enormous mountain to climb, and we are still inventing the necessary equipment to achieve success. Perhaps our vision seems too idealistic, too remote from what is currently happening. If this is so, then the bully has won. Unless all of us muster the courage to face this terrible bully, make the commitment to resolutely confront it, and seek the skills to know what to do, we have already lost.

Educators must provide wounded children with a view of optimism and hope so they can make healthier choices. In some cases, we must renew our own hope, leaving cynicism outside the school's doors. We can and must make a difference by offering students a core set of nonviolent, educationally relevant values. We must model less violent choices and behaviors and teach the skills needed to make responsible nonviolent choices. Maybe no one can do this all of the time, but all of us can do it some of the time. Please join us.

Bibliography

Apelstein, C.D. (1994). *The Gus Chronicles: Reflections from an Abused Kid*. Needham, Mass.: Albert Trieschman Center.

Armstrong, T. (1994). *Multiple Intelligences in the Classroom*. Alexandria, Va.: Association for Supervision and Curriculum Development.

Armstrong, T. (1993). *Seven Kinds of Smart: Identifying and Developing Your Many Intelligences*. New York: NAL Dutton.

Benson, H. (1976). *The Relaxation Response*. New York: Avon.

Brandt, R. (May 1994). "On Educating for Diversity: A Conversation with James A. Banks." *Educational Leadership* 51, 8: 28–31.

Brown, W.K. (1983). *The Other Side of Delinquency*. New Brunswick, N.J.: Rutgers University Press.

Cantrell, M. (Spring 1992). "What We Can Do About Gangs." *Journal of Emotional and Behavioral Problems* 1, 1: 34-37.

Cantrell, R.P., and M.L. Cantrell. (November 1993). "Countering Gang Violence in American Schools." *Principal* 73, 2: 6-9.

Caught in the Crossfire: A Report on Gun Violence in Our Nation's Schools. (1990). Washington, D.C.: Center to Prevent Handgun Violence.

Carnegie Foundation for the Advancement of Teaching with the National Association of Secondary School Principals. (1996). "Breaking Ranks: Changing an American Institution." Reston, Va.: National Association of Secondary School Principals.

CCHR. (1984). *Disorder in Our Public Schools. Report of the Cabinet Council on Human Resources (CCHR)*. Washington, D.C.: U.S. Department of Education, Working Group on School Violence/Discipline.

Charney, R. (Spring 1993). "Teaching Children Nonviolence." *Journal of Emotional and Behavioral Problems* 2, 1: 46-48.

Clinton, H.R. (1996). *It Takes a Village: And Other Lessons Children Teach Us*. New York: Simon & Schuster.

Coles, et al. (1995). *The Ongoing Journey: Awakening Spiritual Life in At-Risk Youth*. Boys Town, Neb.: Boys Town Press.

Colwell, C.G., and S.E. Wigle. (1984). "Applicability of Humor in the Reading/Language Arts Curriculum." *Reading World* 24, 2: 73–80.

"Commissioner's Report to the Education Committees of the Senate and General Assembly on Violence and Vandalism in the Public Schools of New Jersey for the Period July 1, 1987 to June 30, 1988." (1989). Trenton, N.J.: New Jersey State Department of Education.

Coopersmith, S. (1967). *The Antecedents of Self-Esteem*. San Francisco: Freeman Press.

Coopersmith, S. (1975). *Developing Motivation in Young Children*. San Francisco: Albion.

Cuervo, A.G., and J. Lees. (1983). *Delinquency Prevention: An Overview for Policy Development*. Washington, D.C.: Office of Juvenile Justice and Delinquency Prevention.

Curwin, R.L. (1980). "Are Your Students Addicted to Praise?" *Instructor* 90, 3: 61–62.

Curwin, R.L. (1990). *Developing Responsibility and Self-Discipline*. Santa Cruz, Calif.: ETR Associates.

Curwin, R.L. (1992). *Rediscovering Hope: Our Greatest Teaching Strategy*. Bloomington, Ind.: National Education Service.

Curwin, R.L. (November 1993). "The Healing Power of Altruism." *Educational Leadership* 51, 3: 36–39.

Curwin, R.L. (February 1995). "A Humane Approach to Reducing Violence in Schools." *Educational Leadership* 52, 5: 72–75.

Curwin, R.L., and A.N. Mendler. (1988). *Discipline With Dignity*. Alexandria, Va.: Association for Supervision and Curriculum Development.

Curwin, R.L., and A.N. Mendler. (1990). *Am I In Trouble?* Santa Cruz, Calif.: ETR Associates.

Delattre, E.J. (July 1994). "Pushing Against Our Age." *American School Board Journal* 181, 7: 14–18.

Dill, V.S., and M. Haberman. (February 1995). "Building a Gentler School." *Educational Leadership* 52, 5: 69–71.

Donnerstein, E., R. Slaby, and L. Eron. (1992). "Television and Film Violence." Washington, D.C.: American Psychological Association, Commission on Violence and Youth.

Educational Research Service. (1984). "Educators' Views on School Discipline: The Educator Opinion Poll." Arlington, Va.: Author.

Ewing Marion Kauffman Foundation. (1995). "Project Essential: A Research Study." Kansas City, Mo.: Author.

Frisby, D., and J. Beckham. (April 1993). "Dealing with Violence and Threats of Violence in the School." *NASSP Bulletin* 77, 552: 10–15.

Gardner, H. (1983). *Frames of Mind: The Theory of Multiple Intelligences*. New York: Basic Books.

Ginott, H.G. (1976). *Teacher and Child*. New York: Avon.

Goleman, D. (1995). *Emotional Intelligence*. New York: Bantam Books.

Goodlad, J.I. (1984). *A Place Called School: Prospects for the Future*. New York: McGraw-Hill.

Goodlad, J.I. (1994). *Educational Renewal: Better Teachers, Better Schools*. San Francisco: Jossey-Bass.

Grant, J., and F. Capell. (1983). "Reducing School Crime: A Report on the School Team Approach." Nicasio, Calif.: Social Action Research Center.

Hatkoff, A. (1994). "Safety and Children: How Schools Can Help." *Childhood Education* 70, 5: 283–86.

Hechinger, F. (1992). *Fateful Choices: Healthy Youth for the Twenty-First Century.* New York: Hill and Wang.

Herbert, B. (March 3, 1994). "Statistics from the Center to Prevent Handgun Violence" cited in the San Francisco Chronicle, Bob Herbert (reprinted from the NY Times), March 3, 1994 p. A23.

Hiatt, D.B. (1987). *Avenue to Safe Schools: Research, Policy and Practice.* Malibu, Calif.: California Educational Research Association.

Hoover, J.H., and K. Juul. (Spring 1993). "Bullying in Europe and the United States." *Journal of Emotional and Behavioral Problems* 2, 1: 25–29.

Hranitz, J.R., and E.A. Eddowes. (Fall 1990). "Violence: A Crisis in Homes and Schools." *Childhood Education* 67, 1: 4–7.

Johnson, D.W., and R.T. Johnson. (February 1995). "Why Violence Prevention Programs Don't Work—And What Does." *Educational Leadership* 52, 5: 63–67.

Johnson, L. (1992). *My Posse Don't Do Homework.* New York: St. Martin's.

Jung, C.G. (1959). *The Basic Writings of C.G. Jung.* New York: Random House.

Kessler, A. (November 1993). "Peaceful Solutions to Violence." *Principal* 73, 2: 10–12.

Kingrey, P. (1990). *Town and Country Violence.* Encino, Calif.: National School Safety Center.

Knapp, J. (April 1993). "Violence in Children's Lives: Addressing the American Tragedy." *PTA Today* 18, 5: 5–8.

Kohn, A. (1993). *Punished by Rewards: The Trouble with Gold Stars, Incentive Plans, A's, Praise, and Other Bribes.* Boston: Houghton Mifflin.

Kuykendall, C. (1992). *From Rage to Hope: Strategies for Reclaiming Black and Hispanic Youth.* Bloomington Ind.: National Educational Service.

Lazear, D. (1991). *Seven Ways of Knowing: Teaching for Multiple Intelligences.* Palatine Ill.: Skylight Publications.

Licitra, A. (August 11, 1993). "Youth Violence Rampant But Preventable Psychologists Say." *Education Daily*, p. 5.

Liebert, R.M., and J. Sprafkin. (1988). *The Early Window: Effects of Television on Children and Youth.* 3rd ed. New York: Pergamon.

Lifton, B.J. (1988). *The King Of Children: A Biography of Janusz Korczak.* New York: Farrar, Straus and Giroux.

Long, N., and W. Morse. (1996). *Conflict in the Classroom: The Education of At-Risk and Troubled Students.* Austin, Tex.: Pro-Ed.

Maeroff, G.I. (1996). Breaking Ranks: Changing An American Institution. Reston, Va.: National Association of Secondary School Principals and Carnegie Foundation, Commission on the Restructuring of the American High School.

Mansfield, W., and E. Farris. (1992). *Public School Principal Survey on Safe, Disciplined, and Drug-Free Schools.* Washington, D.C.: U.S. Department of

Education, Office of Educational Research and Improvement, National Center for Education Statistics.

Mendler, A.N. (1990). *Smiling At Yourself.* Santa Cruz, Calif.: ETR Associates.

Mendler, A.N. (1992). *What Do I Do When? How to Achieve Discipline with Dignity in the Classroom.* Bloomington, Ind.: National Education Service.

Mendler, A.N. (Summer 1994). "Teaching Hard-To-Reach Youth." *Journal of Emotional and Behavioral Problems* 3, 2: 23–24.

Mendler, A.N. (Fall 1994). "Behavior Management in the Inclusive Classroom." *Journal of Emotional and Behavioral Problems* 3, 3: 59–60.

Mendler, A.N. (Spring 1995). "Classroom Counteraggression: Reclaiming Children and Youth." *Journal of Emotional and Behavioral Problems* 4, 1: 16–17.

Mendler, A.N. (January/February 1996). "Discipline With Dignity: An Approach for the Nineties." *Learning* 24, 4: 16–17.

Milavsky, J.R., R.C. Kessler, H.H. Stipp, and W.S. Rubens. (1992). *Television and Aggression: A Panel Study.* New York: Academic Press.

Molnar, A., and B. Lindquist. (1989). *Changing Problem Behavior in Schools.* San Francisco: Jossey-Bass.

Muir, E. (1990). "Report of the School Safety Department for the 1989-90 School Year." New York: United Federation of Teachers.

Murray, J. (n.d.). "Impact of Televised Violence." Kansas State University. Http://www.ksu.edu/humec/impact.htm

Natale, J. (March 1994). "Roots of Violence." *American School Board Journal* 181, 3: 33-35, 38-40.

National Ethos Survey. (1996). Percept Group, Inc. Http://www.perceptnet. com/natlethos.htm

Nazario, S. (October 7, 1991). "Education: Relaxation Classes Rile Many Parents." *Wall Street Journal*, p. 2-1.

Nebgen, M. (October 1990). "Safe Streets in Tacoma." *American School Board Journal* 177, 10: 26–27.

Nelson, C.M., and R.E. Shores. (Spring 1994). "Dealing with Aggressive and Violent Students." *Preventing School Failure* 38, 3: 5-6.

The 1988 Nielson Report on Television. (1988). Northbrook, Ill.: A.C. Nielson and Company.

Paik, H., and G. Comstock. (August 1994). "The Effects of Television Violence on Antisocial Behavior: A Meta-analysis." *Communication Research* 21, 4: 516–546.

Palmer, E.L. (1988). *Television and America's Children: A Crisis of Neglect.* New York: Oxford University Press.

Parker, K. (February 27, 1996). "School Uniforms: A Way to Put Content Over Style." *USA Today*, p. 11A.

Peach, L., and others. (February 13–16, 1991). "A Study of Violence and Misconduct Perpetrated Against Teachers by Students in Selected Rural

Tennessee Schools." Paper presented at the annual meeting of the Eastern Educational Research Association, Boston, Mass.

Pransky, J. (1991). *Prevention: The Critical Need*. Burlington, Vt.: Burrell Foundation.

Reclaiming Childhood: Responsible Solutions to TV Violence and our Children. (1993). Toronto: Hinks Institute.

Reiss, Jr., A.J., and J.A. Roth, eds. (1993). *Understanding and Preventing Violence*. Washington, D.C.: National Academy Press.

Rochester Democrat and Chronicle and *Rochester Times Union*. (September 1996). "Make Us Safe," a series on local youth violence.

Rochester Research Group. (Spring 1996). "Teens Talk About Violence." A poll conducted for the *Rochester Democrat and Chronicle* and *Rochester Times Union*, WXXI radio and television, and WOKR-TV. Rochester, NY.

Scherer, J., and J. Stimson. (March 1984). "Is School Violence a Serious Concern?" *School Administrator* 41, 3: 19–20, 54.

Shepherd, K.K. (April 1994). "Stemming Conflict Through Peer Mediation." *School Administrator* 51, 4: 14–17.

Stein, A.H., and L.K. Friedrich. (1992). "Television Content and Young Children's Behavior." *Television and Social Behavior*. United States Government Printing Office, Washington, D.C.

Stepp, L.S. (December 7, 1992). "Girl Victims of Bullies are Increasing." *Washington Post*, p. C5.

Toby, J. (Winter 1994). "Everyday School Violence: How Disorder Fuels It." *The American Educator*. 17, 4: 4–9, 44–48.

Trump, K.S. (July 1993). "Tell Teen Gangs: School's Out." *American School Board Journal* 180, 7: 39–42.

Vance, C.M. (1987). "A Comparative Study on the Use of Humor in the Design of Instruction." *Instructional Science* 16, 1: 79–100.

Watson, R.A. (February 1995). "Guide to Violence Prevention." *Educational Leadership* 52, 5: 57–59.

Whitmer, J.E. (1986). "Pickles Will Kill You: Use Humorous Literature to Teach Critical Reading." *Reading Teacher* 39, 6: 530–534.

Wlodkowski, R., and M. Ginsberg. (1995). *Diversity and Motivation*. San Francisco: Jossey-Bass.

Wlodkowski, R.J., and J.H. Jaynes. (1990). *Eager to Learn: Helping Children Become Motivated and Love Learning*. San Francisco: Jossey-Bass.

Wood, W., F.Y. Wong, and J.G. Chachere. (1991). "Effects of Media Violence on Viewers' Aggression in Unconstrained Social Interaction." *Psychological Bulletin* 109, 3: 371-383.

Zahn-Wexler, C., and M. Radke-Yarrow. (1982). "The Development of Altruism: Alternative Research Strategies." *In The Development Of Prosocial Behavior in Young Children*, edited by N. Eisenberg-Berg. New York: Academic Press.

About the Authors

Richard Curwin is a professional teacher, consultant, seminar leader, and author based in San Francisco. His address is 236 West Portal, Box 436, San Francisco, California, 94127. Home: 415-759-6010; Office: 800-772-5227; fax: 415-759-6716.

Allen Mendler is a school psychologist, teacher, educational consultant, and seminar leader based in Rochester, N.Y. His address is P.O. Box 20481, Rochester, N.Y. 14602. Home and fax: 716-427-2659; Office 800-772-5227.

Curwin and Mendler provide staff development, training, courses, and seminars in Discipline With Dignity, Working Successfully With Difficult Students, and Reducing School and Classroom Aggression, Hostility, and Violence. They can be reached by e-mail at: CSMR91F@ Prodigy.com.